STRUCTURED EXERCISES in STRESS MANAGEMENT

A WHOLE PERSON™ HANDBOOK FOR TRAINERS, EDUCATORS AND GROUP LEADERS

VOLUME II

edited by
Nancy Loving Tubesing, EdD
and
Donald A Tubesing, MDiv, PhD

Whole Person Press

Printed in the United States of America
by Port Cities Printing, Superior WI

10   9   8   7   6   5   4   3   2

Published by: **WHOLE PERSON PRESS**
               PO Box 3151
               Duluth MN 55803
               218/728-4077

PREFACE

Two years ago we launched an experiment in health education --
The Whole Person Handbook series of _Structured Exercise in Stress
Management and Wellness Promotion_. We believed then that the
time had come to move beyond peptalks and handouts to an experi-
ential approach that actively involves the participant -- as a
whole person -- in the learning process.

The experiment has been an enormous success! The handbooks have
found their way into the libraries of trainers, consultants,
counselors, teachers, pastors, adult educators, nurses, managers,
group workers, health educators, chaplains, psychologists and
physicians around the world. We're proud that these Volumes have
been a catalyst for dramatic changes in health education.

Volumes II of the Whole Person Handbooks in Stress and Wellness
carry on the tradition of excellence started by their predeces-
sors. Each Handbook contains 36 new structured exercises, complete with step-by-step instructions for easy use. Some utilize
new applications of familiar group processes and techniques.
Others were submitted by people like you who continually strive
to add the creative touch in their teaching. All have been
field-tested with a variety of audiences.

Please note our policy for reproduction of the Handbook contents.
Our purpose in publishing these volumes is to foster interprofes-
sional networking and to provide a framework through which we can
all share out most effective ideas with each other. The layout
is designed for easy photocopying of worksheets and training
notes.

Feel free to adapt and duplicate any sections of the Handbook
for your use in training or educational events -- as long as you
use the proper citation as indicated on the facing paper. However, all materials are still covered by copyright. Prior written permission from Whole Person Press is required if you plan
large-scale reproduction of distribution of any portion of the
Handbook. If you wish to include any material in another publication for sale, please send us your request and proposal.

In the Whole Person Handbook series we've shared our best with
you and hope you'll return the favor. We encourage you to submit your favorite structured exercises for inclusion in future
volumes. You'll find instructions in the contributor's section
at the back of the book. Let us know what works well for you so
that we can carry on the tradition of providing a forum for the
exchange of innovative teaching designs.

Duluth MN   Nancy Loving Tubesing
October 1984   Donald A Tubesing

WHOLE PERSON ASSOCIATES INC
consultants and publishers

specialists in stress and wellness
programs with a whole person focus

CONSULTATION
+ development and implementation of stress management
  and wellness programs for clients around the world
+ curriculum design
+ creative problem solving
+ interdisciplinary think tank

CONTINUING EDUCATION
+ workshops, inservice training, keynote speeches,
  conferences on stress, burnout, wellness, self-
  care, vitality, communication
+ for professional organizations, community-based
  helping agencies, hospitals, business, government,
  education, civic groups

PRODUCT DEVELOPMENT
+ research and development of wellness-oriented
  products for health-conscious businesses and
  institutions
+ design of creative stress management premiums
  and promotions for employees, clients, customers

PUBLISHING
+ Stress and Wellness Handbook series for trainers,
  educators and group leaders
+ innovative training materials, tape and workbook
  packages
+ unique "workshop-in-a-book" self-help guides
+ practical "workshop-in-a-box" cassette tape
  programs
+ unusual relaxation tapes
+ health-related educational games

TABLE OF CONTENTS

ICEBREAKERS

STRESS ASSESSMENTS

MANAGEMENT STRATEGIES

SKILL BUILDERS

ACTION PLANNING/CLOSURE

GROUP ENERGIZERS

INTRODUCTION

Stress is a fact of life -- and from the board room to the emergency room to the living room people are searching for ways to manage stress more positively.

Structured Exercises in Stress Management Volume II offers you 36 designs you can use for helping people move beyond information to implementation. Each exercise is structured to creatively involve people in the learning process, whatever the setting and time constraints, whatever the sophistication of the audience. To aid you in the selection of appropriate exercises, they are grouped into six broad categories:

Icebreakers: These short (10-20 minutes) and lively exercises are designed to introduce people to each other and to the subject of stress management. Try combining an icebreaker with an exercise from the assessment or management section for an instant evening program.

Stress Assessments: These exercises explore the symptoms, sources and dynamics of stress. All six processes help people examine the impact of stress in their lives. You'll find a mixture of shorter assessments (30-60 minutes) and major theme developers (60-90 minutes). Any exercise can easily be contracted or expanded to fit your purpose.

Management Strategies: Each of these five processes focuses on general strategies for dealing with the stress of life. Participants evaluate their coping patterns and explore new alternatives for managing stress.

Skill Builders: Each volume in the Handbook series will focus on a few coping skills in more depth. The five exercises in this section highlight altering perceptions, assertiveness, affirmation, relaxation responses, and time management.

Action Planning/Closure: These five exercises help participants draw together their insights and determine actions they wish to take on their own behalf. One provides between-session homework, another includes a commendation ritual that brings closure to the group process.

Energizers: The ten energizers are designed to perk up the group whenever fatigue sets in. Sprinkle them throughout your program to illustrate skills or concepts. Try one for a change of pace -- everyone's juices (including yours!) will be flowing again in 5-10 minutes.

The Handbook format is designed for easy use. You'll find that
each exercise is described completely, including:

- goals
- group size
- time frame
- materials needed
- step-by-step process instructions
- variations

Special instructions to the trainer are typed in italics.
Scripts to be read to the group are typed in a sans serif face.
Questions to ask the group are preceded by a □.
Mini-lecture notes are preceded by a ● or a *.

The instructions are written primarily for large group (30-100
people) workshop settings, but most of the exercises work just
as well with small groups, in individual therapy and for personal
reflection.

If you are teaching in the workshop or large group setting, we
believe that the use of small discussion groups is the most
potent learning structure available to you. We've found that
groups of four person each provide ample "air time" and a good
variety of interaction. Let groups meet together two or three
different times before forming new groups.

These personal "sharing groups" allow people to make positive
contact with each other and encourage them to personalize their
experience in depth. On evaluations, some people will say "Drop
this," others will say, "Give us more small group time," but
most will report that the time you give them to share with each
other becomes the heart of the workshop.

If you are working with an intact group of 12 people or less,
you may at times want to keep the whole group together for process and discussion time rather than divide into the suggested
four or six person groups.

Each trainer has personal strengths, biases, pet concepts and
processes. We expect and encourage you to expand and modify
what you find here to accommodate your style. Adjust the exercises as you see fit. Bring these designs to life for your
participants by inserting your own content and examples into
your teaching. Experiment!

And when you come up with something new, let us know . . .

ICEBREAKERS

37 INTRODUCTIONS IV

In these three quick icebreakers, participants introduce
themselves with name-matching copers (ALPHABET COPERS),
share their reasons for attending the course (PERSONAL/
PROFESSIONAL) and articulate their stress management
"wishes" (WAVE THE MAGIC WAND).

GOALS

1) To get acquainted.

2) To heighten awareness of personal goals.

GROUP SIZE

Unlimited; some adjustments may be necessary with very
large or very small groups.

TIME FRAME

10-20 minutes

PROCESS

ALPHABET COPERS

1) The trainer invites participants to introduce them-
    selves to the group in a memorable way. Each person
    must think of a coping technique that could be used to
    manage stress -- that also begins with the same first
    letter as her first or last name.

    *Note: The trainer may need to prime the pump with a few
          examples (eg, "I'm Sally Thomas and my coper
          is smoking or talking about it.") Be sure to
          include both "positive" and "negative" copers in
          your examples. Allow people a minute or two to
          think of a good self-introduction.*

2) Participants introduce themselves one by one, stating
    their names and the matching coper.

    *Note: With more than 20 people, divide into smaller
          groups (8-16) for this exercise.*

VARIATION

■ After Step 2, the trainer could challenge the group to see
  how quickly they can learn everyone's name using the companion copers as cues.

PERSONAL/PROFESSIONAL

1) The trainer invites participants to focus on their reasons for coming to the session/workshop, noting that most people sign up for stress management courses with mixed motivations -- anticipating they will be able to apply what they learn to their personal life as well as to their job situation.

2) One-by-one participants introduce themselves to others in the group and share their responses to the following sentence stems:
   * One thing I'm hoping to gain <u>personally</u> from this meeting . . .
   * One thing I'm hoping to gain <u>professionally</u> (or for my job situation) . . .

   Note: If the group is larger than 20 participants, form smaller groups of 6-12 persons for the introductions.

3) The trainer summarizes the expectations implicit in participants' introductions and highlights the similarity/variety of reasons that motivate participation.

   Note: PERSONAL/PROFESSIONAL REVIEW (p 97) would be especially appropriate as a closing exercise when this process is used as an icebreaker.

WAVE THE MAGIC WAND

1) The trainer invites participants to imagine they have a fairy godmother who can wave her magic wand and grant any wish they make regarding their life stress or coping style. Each person is to consider his current life situation and decide what stress management "wish" he would like granted.

   Note: The trainer may want to give several examples of stress management "wishes." (eg, "I wish I could stop worrying so much," "I'd like to be able to laugh at myself more," "I wish someone would take off all the pressure," "I need help meeting deadlines," "Get my boss off my back," "Stop all the arguments at home," "Keep my kids out of trouble," etc). The "wishes" do not have to be practical or logical.

© 1984   Whole Person Press   PO Box 3151   Duluth MN 55803

2)   Participants introduce themselves to others in the
     group by stating what "wish" for improving their stress
     level or coping capacity they would want their fairy
     godmother to grant them.

     *Note: With groups larger than 20, divide participants
            into smaller units of 6-10 for these introductions.*

VARIATION

▪ This process could be used effectively as a feedback and
  closure exercise at the end of a workshop. Participants
  would then "wave their magic wands" for one another, telling
  each group member how they imagine he will manage his stress
  more positively.

TRAINER'S NOTES

TRAINER'S NOTES

38 TORTOISE, HARE OR THOROUGHBRED?

In this energizing mixer participants take on the identity
of the animal whose life patterns most closely resemble
their own. These "habitat" groups discuss the eustress and
distress caused by their lifestyle.

GOALS

1) To affirm personal lifestyle patterns.

2) To identify lifestyle-related eustress and distress.

3) To promote interaction among participants.

GROUP SIZE

15-40 works best.

TIME FRAME

20-30 minutes; more with larger groups.

MATERIALS NEEDED

Newsprint posters labeled "Tortoise", "Hare" and
"Thoroughbred."

PROCESS

1) The trainer introduces the exercise by noting some or
    all of the following points:

    • Over time people develop a lifestyle pattern that
      works for them. Some folks go at a slow and steady
      pace, others hop around from crisis to crisis or
      challenge to challenge. Still others seem to race
      through life in high gear taking everything in
      stride.

    • There is nothing intrinsically "right" or "wrong"
      about any of these lifestyle patterns. Each has
      its own stresses and strains, joys and rewards.

    • Hans Selye, one of the pioneer stress researchers
      suggests that the key to effective stress manage-
      ment is to find out which pattern fits you -- and
      then live it!

2) The trainer invites participants to consider their own

typical life patterns, comparing them to the mythical
tortoise, hare and thoroughbred. As the trainer reads
the descriptions, each participant decides which of the
animals she resembles most.

- TORTOISE:

    Likes to move ahead slowly and steadily.
    Doesn't let others rush her.
    Finds strength from pulling in her head.
    Has a strong protective shell.
    Doesn't take unnecessary risks.
    Prefers life on an even keel without crisis.
    Paces herself, takes one thing at a time.

- HARE:

    Moves with quick starts and stops.
    Produces well under pressure.
    Finds strength in exploration and challenge.
    Is fragile, agile and lucky.
    Enjoys risks and adventures.
    Hops from crisis to crisis, is easily distracted.
    Always has many irons in the fire.

- THOROUGHBRED:

    Economy and grace of movement.
    Varies pace according to situation.
    Strength comes from top-flight conditioning.
    Always under control.
    Thrives on competition and challenge.
    Has clear goals with mileposts to mark progress
        along the way.
    Always has something left for the stretch.

3) The trainer designates separate areas of the room as
    "habitats" for the three animals, using newsprint posters
    to designate which is which. Participants move to the
    "habitat" of the animal whose lifestyle description
    most closely resembles their own.

    *Note: The trainer may need to read the descriptions a
        second time and insist that the "mixed breeds"
        make a choice, even if they don't fit perfectly
        in any category. Can you imagine these animals
        cross-mating?!?!*

4) In each animal group, participants introduce themselves
    by stating what influenced them to choose this group.

    When everyone in the group is introduced, participants

list on the left side of the newsprint all the real and
potential positive benefits (eustress) of their lifestyle -- the joys, delights, rewards, etc of being a
tortoise, hare or thoroughbred. On the right side
they make a list of all the real and potential negative
side effects (distress) of their lifestyle.

5)   The trainer reconvenes the total group and asks for
comments, insights and observations. If the idea
doesn't arise spontaneously, the trainer should remind
the group how important it is for each person to
respect, rather than resist, her own pattern.

VARIATION

■ For adventuresome people, after Step 4 the trainer may
instruct the three groups to race around the room <u>as a group</u>
at the pace, and with the "style" of their animal. Allow
two minutes for planning, then give the starting signal.

TRAINER'S NOTES

TRAINER'S NOTES

39 FOUR QUADRANT QUESTIONS

In the first segment of this two-part exercise participants
get acquainted in small groups as they explore stress management styles. In the follow-up meeting at the session's
end, group members answer their own questions about stress.

GOALS

1) To help participants identify their personal stress
   management style.

2) To reinforce the value of mutual responsibility for
   learning.

3) To promote interaction and mutual respect among participants.

GROUP SIZE

Unlimited; works well with large groups if the space is
adequate.

TIME FRAME

Part I, 15-20 minutes; Part II, 10-15 minutes.

MATERIALS NEEDED

Blank paper

PROCESS

1) The trainer announces that he is going
   to be asking four questions to be
   answered briefly in writing. Participants are instructed to divide a blank
   sheet of paper into four quadrants.

I	II
III	IV

In Quadrant I, the trainer asks participants to respond
to the following questions:

☐ Think of a person you know who manages stress extremely well. Write down that person's name.
☐ What qualities (skills, attitudes, behaviors) make
  this person such a good stress manager?

The trainer invites people to think about their own
style of managing stress. In Quadrant II participants
reply to the question:

◻ Describe your personal stress management style.
What are your strong/weak coping skills? How do
you tackle stressful situations?

The trainer directs participants to review their day so
far, and in Quadrant III to answer one of the following
questions:

◻ In what ways did you experience stress in coming to
this session today? OR
◻ How have you experienced stress so far in this session?

In Quadrant IV, participants respond to the inquiry:

◻ What's one question you have about stress?

2) The trainer directs participants to find a partner.
Once everyone is paired off, partners share their answers from Quadrant III -- how they experienced stress
today. (2-3 minutes)

3) The trainer asks each duo to join with another pair,
making foursomes. In this expanded small group, participants discuss their responses from Quadrants I and
II.

The trainer sets the "batting order" by directing that
sharing proceed in alphabetical order, starting with
the person whose first name is closest to A. Participants are encouraged to elaborate their answers as much
as they want, and whenever they feel "dry" to pass the
spotlight to the next person. When everyone is finished
the group should spend the remaining time comparing,
contrasting and expanding their insights. (10 minutes)

4) The trainer reconvenes the group and comments that this
exercise has offered an opportunity for participants to
clarify their own thinking and expand each others'
understanding of stress. He indicates that discussion
of the questions in the fourth quadrant will be saved
until later in the session. The trainer proceeds with
the major content portion of the course.

5) At some point near the end of the session (or course),
after participants have received the essential content
on stress and stress management, the trainer instructs
people to rejoin the small groups established for the
first part of this exercise.

One-by-one, participants ask the questions they had
written in Quadrant IV. The group discusses possible

answers to each question, based on what they have
learned during the session.

6) The trainer reconvenes the large group and asks for
    examples of questions and answers generated by the
    small groups. He uses these as a springboard for
    expanding, clarifying and summarizing the session
    content.

TRAINER'S NOTES

We first learned this process from Joel Goodman.

© 1984 Whole Person Press   PO Box 3151   Duluth MN 55803

40 LIFE EVENT BINGO

Participants use the Social Readjustment Rating Scale life events as a bingo card in this get-acquainted exercise.

GOALS

1) To discover the diversity of coping techniques people use in dealing with stressful life events.

2) To introduce the group to each other and to the topic in an entertaining manner.

GROUP SIZE

Best with groups of 15-20 or more persons.

TIME FRAME

10-20 minutes

MATERIALS NEEDED

"Life Event Bingo" worksheets for all participants.

PROCESS

1) The trainer distributes the Bingo sheets and invites participants to move around in the group, introducing themselves and searching for individuals who have experienced each life event within the past year. When a participant finds someone who has experienced a particular event, she interviews him to find out what coping technique was most useful to him in dealing with that change. She then writes the person's name and most effective copers in the appropriate space and moves on to meet a new person who coped with a different life change in the past year.

> *Note: Depending on the time available, play "5-in-a-row" or "full-card" Bingo, or stop the process whenever people have experienced a significant exchange of information. Remind participants that their emphasis should be on making contact with others in the group and learning about the variety of coping skills people (including themselves) use in response to potentially stressful situations. Filling the Bingo card is only a secondary goal!*

2) The trainer reconvenes the group and asks what they learned about stress, change, coping and each other.

LIFE EVENT BINGO

Find someone here who has experienced these life events during the past year. Ask that person to describe the coping technique that worked best for them in that situation and write the coper in the appropriate box. Try to find a different person for each event.

divorce	death of spouse	business readjust-ment	starting/stopping school	change in work responsibilities
change in financial status	son/daughter leaves home	jail term	death of a close friend	added someone to the family
change in personal habits	retirement	outstanding per-sonal achievement	personal illness/injury	more arguments with spouse
pregnancy	change in resi-dence	change in working hours/conditions	fired at work	death of close family member
change to differ-ent line of work	trouble with the in-laws	sickness in family	marriage	took out a mortgage

41 **EXCLUSIVE INTERVIEW**

Participants get acquainted by pairing up for in-depth interviews on stress and coping skills.

GOALS

1) To explore personal stress management styles.

2) To provide an initial bonding experience that models
    personal sharing and peer support.

GROUP SIZE

Unlimited

TIME FRAME

25-30 minutes; could be shortened with some loss of depth.

MATERIALS NEEDED

"Leading Questions" handout for everyone

PROCESS

1) The trainer distributes the "Leading Questions" handout
    and announces that everyone is going to have an oppor-
    tunity to play the role of "cub reporter" interviewing
    a local "celebrity".

2) Participants are asked to choose a partner (preferably
    someone they don't know well) and move to a relatively
    private space in the room. Each pair decides who will
    be the "celebrity" and who will be the "reporter" in the
    first round.

3) The trainer instructs the "reporters" to spend the next
    10 minutes pursuing an in-depth interview of the "cele-
    brity," using whatever leading questions from the hand-
    out seem appropriate. The goal of the interview is to
    learn as much as possible about the "celebrity's" stress
    patterns and coping style.

    "Celebrities" answer the questions as completely as they
    feel comfortable, keeping in mind the goal of getting a
    new perspective on their own stress management patterns.
    After 10 minutes, the trainer asks all "reporters" to
    write down a "lead sentence" for their article about
    the "celebrity" they interviewed.

> *Note: The trainer may want to give some examples, such as, "Moving has never bothered Tom Marcus -- he's an expert at instant relationships." Or "Susan Antwerp's favorite coping technique is an oatmeal facial." Or "Quit hoping . . . start coping. That's Amelia Winter's advice for the stressed." Remind reporters to use the celebrity's name in the sentence.*

4) "Reporters" and "celebrities" switch roles for the second 10-minute interview. At the end of the interview, the "reporter" writes a lead sentence.

5) The trainer suggests that partners briefly discuss their reactions to the process and what they learned about themselves.

6) The trainer reconvenes the whole group and asks participants to introduce their partners by reading their lead sentences.

VARIATIONS

- The trainer could conduct "group interviews" with 6-8 persons at a time. The group to be interviewed forms a circle at the front. The remaining participants "observe" while the trainer facilitates the small group's discussion of one or more leading questions. Several groups could be interviewed in this "fish bowl" fashion, each answering different questions. The trainer may invite onlookers to comment or ask additional questions.

- Instead of pairing up for interviews, participants could divide into small groups (4-8 people) for discussion of one or more leading questions assigned by the trainer.

- This exercise could be expanded into a theme-building chalk talk by asking each participant to choose one question from the list and respond to it in writing. The trainer collects the paragraphs, reads them out loud and elaborates on the issues and concerns raised in the answers.

TRAINER'S NOTES

© 1984   Whole Person Press   PO Box 3151   Duluth MN 55803

LEADING QUESTIONS

How would you define stress?

When do you feel most stressed?

Where in your body do you feel stress?

What people in your life cause you stress?

How do you feel before, during and after a stressful situation?

What situations do you "breeze through" that seem stressful to others?

In what ways is stress "good" for you?

What are some of the special stressors that go along with different life stages?

What coping skills have you found the most helpful in dealing with stress?

What situation is extremely stressful to you, but doesn't seem to bother other people?

What is the key ingredient in stress management?

What advice would you give someone about the best way to manage stress?

What's the most stressful life experience you can imagine? Why would it be so stressful?

What has been the most stressful period in your life so far? What skills did you use to deal with it?

How do/did your parents deal with stress?

What's the biggest source of stress for you at work?

STRESS ASSESSMENTS

42 THE FOURTH SOURCE OF STRESS (p 17)

This exercise points out the role that poor self-esteem plays in creating distress, and helps participants become aware of the power of positive self-esteem as a primary stress management tool. (45-60 minutes)

43 BURNOUT INDEX (p 25)

Using this quick checklist of stress-related symptoms, participants may ascertain their level of stress as well as the likelihood that they will experience burnout. (10-15 minutes)

44 DRAGNET (p 28)

In this stress assessment participants "unravel the mystery" of their stress by recording the facts and analyzing the clues they uncover. (30-40 minutes)

45 BACK TO THE DRAWING BOARD (p 32)

In this major exercise participants analyze the drainers and energizers of their work environment by drawing a symbolic picture of their work setting. (50-75 minutes)

45 LIFETRAP II: HOOKED ON HELPING (p 36)

Participants affirm the admirable nature of their caring for others and also examine the long-term stress and resulting exhaustion that is inevitable when care-giving becomes an addiction. Although this extended, multi-process exercise is designed for "professional" helpers (nurses, counselors, clergy, teachers, etc), the issues apply to all caring people — especially working parents. (60-90 minutes)

47 CIRCUIT OVERLOAD (p 46)

This assessment tool helps participants to see how much stress they are currently "loading on the circuits." (15-20 minutes)

42 THE FOURTH SOURCE OF STRESS

This exercise points out the role that poor self-esteem plays in creating distress, and helps participants become aware of the power of positive self-esteem as a primary stress management tool.

GOALS

1) To acknowledge poor self-esteem as the primary and most common source of distress.

2) To understand the importance of positive self-esteem in the management of day-to-day stress.

3) To help participants assess and improve their opinion of themselves.

GROUP SIZE

Unlimited

TIME FRAME

45-60 minutes

MATERIALS NEEDED

One copy of the "Self-Esteem Checklist" and "Messages From My Past" worksheets for each participant.

PROCESS

Note: This exercise is divided into five sequential segments which could be used independently or in some other combination. LIFE EVENT BINGO (p 12) would fit well as a warm-up.

A) The Sources of Stress -- chalk talk (15-20 minutes)
B) Self-Esteem as the Key -- chalk talk (5-10 minutes)
C) Assessing Self-Esteem -- checklist (10-15 minutes)
D) The Origins of Self-Esteem - worksheet (10-15 minutes)
E) Improving Self-Esteem -- practice suggestions (5-10 minutes)

A) <u>The Sources of Stress</u>

1) The trainer outlines the four major sources of stress according to the following model:

● Customary, anticipated life events. These events represent the transitions of normal life (eg, graduating from high school or college, marriage, having children, moving to a new home, changing jobs, retiring, etc).

They can be influenced, but not totally controlled, by personal decisions. Normally, they cause a positive, stimulating form of stress. Symptoms of distress may be experienced when several of these events cluster in a short time period or when we resist the changes represented by the events.

● Unexpected life events. These events are the "tragedies" and "shocks" of life (eg, being involved in an accident, being the victim of a crime, the sudden death of a loved one, losing one's job, etc).

These stressors usually occur to us suddenly, without warning, and are not in our control. The stress symptoms that result are also often sudden, and sometimes severe. Normally, however, such symptoms do not become chronic. With time we heal and the symptoms are relieved.

● Progressive accumulating events. These represent the everyday strains of life, especially unresolved stressors in close relationships (eg, ongoing conflict with spouse, continuing parent-child friction, long-term care for a disabled relative, boredom with a career path, cumulative job-related pressures, etc).

The symptoms of stress-exhaustion resulting from these factors develop slowly, but because they accumulate over time, they are not easily dissipated. The magnitude of these pressures often seem to gain momentum, as the "victims" feel increasingly worn out and unable to cope.

● Personal trait stress. This self-imposed stress caused by perfectionism, insecurity, lack of self confidence, feelings of jealousy or inadequacy, is the only source of stress over which we have total control.

Stress caused by low self-esteem pervades all daily situations and influences all interactions. Sufferers often become anxious worriers, plagued by generalized feelings of fear and dis-ease. These symptoms are often chronic and life-long unless the source of the stress -- negative feelings about self -- is changed.

2) The trainer may ask participants, individually or as a
    group, to identify their predominant sources of stress
    based on this paradigm. A discussion of their findings
    may follow.

B) Self-Esteem as the Key

3) The trainer outlines the role of self-esteem by sharing
    the following thoughts:

    ● "Love your neighbor as yourself" is a saying fam-
      iliar to most of us. It means that you must have
      the capacity to love and accept yourself in order
      to form and keep satisfying relationships with
      others. Self-esteem means accepting yourself for
      who you really are, and believing that you are
      indeed a worthwhile person who is deserving of
      love and respect from others.

    ● Self-esteem is our sense of how good we feel about
      ourselves. It is based on our judgment of our-
      selves, not on other people's assessment. Our self-
      esteem does not depend on our talent. Some very
      ordinary people feel very good about themselves,
      while other extra-ordinary high achievers hold low
      opinions of themselves.

    ● Self-esteem is the primary key to long-term stress
      management. Why? The first three sources of stress
      (predictable life events, unexpected changes and
      the buildup of daily strains) are much easier to
      handle when we believe in ourselves. A positive,
      healthy self-esteem gives us the "hardiness" to roll
      with the punches" of life, and to see them as chal-
      lenges to be met, rather than threats to be feared.

    ● The fourth category of stressors is entirely the
      result of a low self-esteem. It's this category of
      stress that is most pervasive and exhausting over
      the long run. Personal trait stress cannot be over-
      come, or even altered, until the self-esteem prob-
      lems that cause it are corrected.

4) The trainer solicits from the group examples of people
    they know (including themselves!) whose self-esteem has
    contributed to their stress or limited their coping
    capabilities. She then asks for illustrations of people
    whose healthy self-esteem has had a positive impact on
    their stress management capacity.

C) Assessing Self-Esteem

5) The trainer instructs participants to complete the
"Self-Esteem Checklist" by marking their response to
each of the fourteen questions.

6) Participants pair up with a partner. The trainer then
asks participants to share their responses to the following questions.

   □ In what ways does your self-esteem make you more
   vulnerable to stress?
   □ In what ways does your self-esteem contribute to
   your "hardiness" and your ability to deal with
   life's stressors?
   □ How do you feel about your current level of self-
   esteem?
   □ How might you increase your "hardiness" by improving
   your self-esteem?

D) The Origins of Self-Esteem

7) The trainer points out to participants that the first
step in improving their image of themselves is to gain
an awareness of the roots of their current self-esteem.
Participants then complete the "Messages From My Past"
worksheet. (5 minutes)

8) Partners share their answers and discuss any insights
that occur to them. (5 minutes)

   Note: The trainer may also ask participants to compare
         their responses to the following questions:
         □ What patterns or themes do you notice in your
           messages from the past?
         □ Are these messages accurate descriptions of
           you today?
         □ Which need revision? Which could/should be
           discarded? Which do you cherish?

9) The trainer challenges the group by observing:

   * "What we are may be our parents' fault, what we
   remain is our responsibility!"
   * "Be sure you are not handicapping yourself with low
   self-esteem, just because of someone's ill-timed
   remark years ago."

E) Improving Self-Esteem

  10) The trainer may offer some or all of the following sug-
      gestions for taking the first steps toward improving
      personal self-esteem.

      • Speak up for yourself. Your opinion is valid. No
        one can "put you down" unless you "put them up" by
        deciding their viewpoint is worth more than yours.
        Resist such belittling thoughts.

      • Don't put yourself down. Nobody's perfect. Mis-
        takes and failures are a normal component of life
        -- welcome to the human race! Instead of criticizing
        yourself, forgive yourself.

      • Remember -- you're in charge of your life. Think for
        yourself! Make your own decisions! Trust your
        process!

      • Get off the pity pot. Don't indulge in guilt trips
        or blaming and shaming routines.

      • Believe in yourself. Stop counting on others to tell
        you that you count. Tell yourself!

      • Be all that you can be. Don't depend on others to
        do things for you that you are capable of doing for
        yourself -- even if they could do a better job!

      • Tend to your needs. Don't neglect yourself or sub-
        vert your needs in order to meet the needs of others.

      • Be proud of yourself. You are unique and your very
        existence proves your innate worth. Don't forget it!

  11) The trainer concludes the exercise by inviting partici-
      pants to describe whatever insights have occurred to
      them during the process. Participants may also share
      any personal resolutions for improving their self-esteem.

VARIATION

  ■ This exercise could be expanded to include an in-depth ex-
    ploration of all four sources of stress. As part of Step 1
    the trainer presents additional information on life events
    stress, using the Holmes and Rahe "Social Readjustment
    Rating Scale" as an assessment tool. Participants complete
    the scale for themselves, then decide as a group which items
    fall in the "anticipated" category and which in the "unex-
    pected" category. The trainer solicits examples of the
    third source of stress -- accumulated unresolved stressors
    and strain -- before moving on to highlight personal trait
    stress.

SELF-ESTEEM CHECKLIST

	ALMOST ALWAYS	OFTEN	RARELY	NEVER
1) Do you find yourself bragging or exaggerating the importance of your role?	___	___	___	___
2) Are you jealous of the possessions, opportunities or positions of others?	___	___	___	___
3) Do you find yourself judging your behavior by other people's standards or expectations rather than your own?	___	___	___	___
4) Are you possessive in your relationships with friends and/or family members?	___	___	___	___
5) Is it difficult for you to acknowledge your own mistakes?	___	___	___	___
6) Do you resort to bullying and intimidation in your dealings with others?	___	___	___	___
7) Do you "put people down" so that you can feel "one up?"	___	___	___	___
8) Are you a perfectionist?	___	___	___	___
9) Must you be a "winner" in recreational activities in order to have fun?	___	___	___	___
10) When faced with new opportunities do you feel inadequate or insecure?	___	___	___	___
11) Do you have difficulty accepting compliments?	___	___	___	___
12) Do you refrain from expressing your feelings and opinions?	___	___	___	___
13) Do you shy away from trying new things for fear of failure or looking dumb?	___	___	___	___
14) Do you neglect your own needs in order to respond to the needs of others?	___	___	___	___

"ALMOST ALWAYS" or "OFTEN" answers to any of these questions may indicate that your level of self-esteem needs attention.

MESSAGES FROM MY PAST

The messages we have received from people who have been important
in our lives contribute to our level of self-esteem. These messages can be positive or negative.

In the space below, write the messages you recall receiving from
people who have been important to you.

Examples:

> *Mother* - *"You're so rattle-brained! You'd lose your head
> if it weren't attached to the rest of you!"*
> *Father* - *"That's my daughter -- she can do just about any-
> thing she sets her mind to."*
> *Teacher* - *"He's not the brightest kid, but he sure tries
> hard."*
> *Others* - *"How are you going to get ahead if your head is
> always in the clouds?"*

MOTHER _____

_____

FATHER _____

_____

SIBLINGS _____

_____

CLERGY _____

_____

FRIENDS _____

_____

TEACHERS _____

_____

COACH _____

_____

OTHERS _____

_____

TRAINER'S NOTES

Submitted by Gloria Singer.
The "Four Sources of Stress" model (Step 1) is summarized from
an article by Barbara Brown ("A Conceptual Analysis of 'The
Stress of Life Phenomenon.'" Stress, II, 1981).
The "Self-Esteem Checklist" is based on a column by Sydney J
Harris.
The suggestions for improving self-esteem (Step 10) are adapted
from Dunlap & Stewart, Keeping the Fire Alive (Tulsa: Penwell
Books, 1983).

43 BURNOUT INDEX

Using this quick checklist of stress-related symptoms, participants may ascertain their level of stress as well as the likelihood that they will experience burnout.

GOALS

1) To assess participants' current level of stress.

2) To indicate that the toll of stress exhaustion is exacted on the whole person, not just the body.

GROUP SIZE

Unlimited; also appropriate for work with individuals.

TIME FRAME

10-15 minutes

MATERIALS NEEDED

"Six Typical Symptoms of Burnout" worksheet for each participant.

PROCESS

1) The trainer introduces the concept that a buildup of stress and strain can lead to burnout. He points out that no one is immune to stress exhaustion, covering some or all of the following points:

- Don't be surprised when you see the signs of stress fatigue in yourself and others -- because you will. Many people feel under stress a good share of the time.

- In an informal survey a remarkable percentage of people in different professions reported that they are usually or always under stress:

  * 80% of executives and managers
  * 66% of teachers and secretaries
  * 67% of farmers
  * 61% of homemakers

- Most burnout symptoms are generalized -- that is, they cannot be traced to one particular stressor. Stress symptoms are signs of <u>overall exhaustion</u>.

Often, therefore, they "just don't make sense" when
we try to understand which of our "problems" has
caused them.

● All of us need to be on guard to prevent burnout.
When the symptoms pop up, don't ignore them -- take
creative action to nip the problem in the bud.

2) Participants complete the "Six Typical Symptoms of
Burnout" worksheet. (5 minutes)

3) The trainer outlines the "Burnout Index" scoring code
for the test.

BURNOUT INDEX

A quick rule of thumb is that a person is close to
burnout when they're experiencing two of these
symptoms, has a severe case with four, and is ter-
minally ill if all six are present!

If you never recognize any of these symptoms in
yourself, ever, you're probably too far gone for
help!

4) The trainer may invite a sharing of observations and
insights from the group.

TRAINER'S NOTES

Submitted by Thomas G Boman

© 1984 Whole Person Press   PO Box 3151   Duluth MN 55803

SIX TYPICAL SYMPTOMS OF BURNOUT

Check any stress exhaustion symptom that you have experienced
lately. Make additional specific notes on symptoms that are
regularly part of your life.

Yes No

☐   ☐   1) Irritability and a general distrust of others'
               intentions.

☐   ☐   2) No new ideas in the past six months.

☐   ☐   3) Lack of energy -- both physical and emotional.

☐   ☐   4) Feelings of isolation and lack of personal support.

☐   ☐   5) Urge to get out of my present job situation.

☐   ☐   6) An attempt to feel good about myself by focusing
               on "how much" I do.

How many symptoms are you currently experiencing? _____

What symptoms, other than those listed, are you experiencing?

_____

_____

Which symptoms concern you the most? (in your own words)
"I am particularly concerned when I begin to feel _____

_____."

Which symptoms would you say are sure signs that if you don't
change something you're headed for big trouble?

_____

_____

Any other observations or comments? _____

_____

_____

44 DRAGNET

In this stress assessment participants "unravel the mystery" of their stress by recording the facts and analyzing the clues they uncover.

GOALS

1) To identify current stressors.

2) To analyze the situational circumstances of each stressor and to discover the common patterns that connect them.

GROUP SIZE

Unlimited, also effective for work with individuals.

TIME FRAME

30-40 minutes

MATERIALS NEEDED

"Dragnet Stress Analysis Worksheet" for each participant.

PROCESS

1) The trainer distributes the worksheets and invites participants to make a list of their current stressors in the left hand column.

2) Participants then "gather the facts" of their stress by answering the What? When? Where? Who? How? Why? questions for each stressor they have listed.

    Note: You're interested in "the facts" only, not long essays. Hence, the space for writing has been limited. Encourage participants to record one or two words in each and every box.

    Participants will probably find that in some columns their answers quickly become repetitious. This is appropriate, and will lead to clues for unraveling the mystery of their current stress dilemma.

3) Participants review their notes in each vertical column and summarize their findings in the space provided at the bottom of the chart.

4)   Participants analyze the facts of their stress by list-
     ing their suspicions and the areas of promise for fur-
     ther investigation.

5)   The trainer divides participants into groups of four
     persons each and instructs them to share with each other
     a summary of the "facts of their case" as well as their
     list of suspicions and areas for further investigation.
     (2-3 minutes each, 15-20 minutes overall)

6)   The trainer reconvenes the entire group and invites
     comments on the themes and insights observed by the
     group.

TRAINER'S NOTES

© 1984   Whole Person Press   PO Box 3151   Duluth MN 55803

DRAGNET STRESS ANALYSIS WORKSHEET

STRESSORS (list 5-8)	WHAT? The situation? The precipitating actions/inter-actions? The result/resolution?	WHEN? Date, time of day? How often? Following what? Preceding what?	WHERE? Location? Work, home, play? Other circumstances?	WHO? Spouse? Children? Friends? Supervisors? Subordinates? Strangers?	HOW? The trigger? The power and force behind it? The style?	WHY? Bad attitude? Dirty politics? Stupidity? Circumstances beyond control?
GATHER THE FACTS						
Summarize the essential ingredient of each column.						

Looking at the clues in this fact-gathering document, the following hunches about my stress mysteries should be investigated further . . .

I suspect that:

I suspect that:

I suspect that:

To unravel the mystery of my current stress, I need to investigate the following options:

I should investigate:

I should investigate:

I should investigate:

45 BACK TO THE DRAWING BOARD

In this major exercise participants analyze the drainers and energizers of their work environment by drawing a symbolic picture of their work setting.

GOALS

1) To recognize factors in the job setting which produce distress.

2) To isolate factors in the job setting which nurture and reward.

3) To identify strategies for coping with organizational, work-related stress.

GROUP SIZE

Unlimited

TIME FRAME

50-75 minutes

MATERIALS NEEDED

Blank paper

PROCESS

1) As a warm-up to this exercise, the trainer directs participants to write a 20-30 word description of the organization in which they work and their specific job. Participants are to leave out all subjective value judgments and cynical comments. The descriptions are to be objective. (5 minutes) For example,

> "I am an RN in charge of labor and delivery at a 500 bed hospital that is currently adding two new wings and three new units."

> "I am in charge of the midwest region, 18-person sales force for a California-based company specializing in designing computer software packages for small businesses."

2) Participants are invited to read their objective paragraphs (6-10 volunteers). The remaining participants listen carefully and note the subtle differences in each description.

*Note: Even when participants are from the same company
the variations in their descriptions are always
interesting, sometimes humorous.*

*The trainer may acknowledge the fact that objec-
tive definitions are difficult to write when
you're so close to, and caught up in, your work.*

3) The trainer distributes blank paper and instructs parti-
    cipants to draw a picture of their organization <u>with
    themselves in it</u>. (10 minutes)

*Note: Assure participants that they need not be artists.
They may use symbols, diagrams, words, organizational charts or characterizations of key people
-- to depict the power issues, allegiances and
relationships that exist. Encourage them to get
started by drawing the first image that comes to
their minds and to then follow their intuitions
as they embellish the picture.*

4) The trainer asks participants to examine their own pic-
    ture and note those factors that are the disturbing,
    frustrating stress-producers -- marking these stressors
    with an exclamation point (!). Participants may also
    wish to add a word or two of explanation at these points

    In addition, the trainer may ask participants to reflect
    on some or all of the following questions and to incor-
    porate their responses into the picture with words,
    symbols or drawings.

    □ What's stressful about your work relationships?
        with peers, subordinates, supervisors, top
        management, customers; the conflicts, lack of
        guidance, competition, jealousy, negativism,
        cynicism.
    □ What's stressful about the way the organization
      works?
        the pressure, the pace, the way decisions are
        made, the flow of information, who gets ahead
        and how, the hidden agendas, the "rules", the
        red tape, the reporting requirements, the job
        descriptions, the business philosophy.
    □ What's stressful about the reward system?
        the pay, the fringes, the appreciation and
        affirmation, the budget cuts, the "perks", the
        parties.
    □ What's stressful about the physical environment?
        the noise level, the equipment, the space.

© 1984 Whole Person Press   PO Box 3151   Duluth MN 55803

What's stressful about the way you fit in and the work you do?

the tasks, the opportunity for growth or advancement, the skills required, the deadlines, the quotas, the number of "hats".

5) The trainer points out that every job and every organization also includes "plusses" -- the positive, pleasant factors that energize us and draw us back. Participants are instructed to examine their pictures and note these supportive, nurturing factors -- marking these energizers with a star (*). Participants may also wish to add a word or two of explanation at these points.

The trainer solicits from the group 25-30 specific examples of organizational nutrients they included in their drawings. Participants embellish their drawings with additional relevant energizers as they are suggested.

If the group gets stuck, the trainer highlights several positive factors that may be present in the workplace:

* Gratitude and thanks -- from peers, supervisors, subordinates, customers.
* Success in completing tasks, clarity in jobs and responsibilities.
* Respect, being listened to, power to make decisions.
* Common purposes, rituals and traditions.
* Good pay, fringes, flexible hours, day care, car pool.
* Stimulation, challenge, new ideas, variety.
* Comfort, windows, music, beautiful grounds.
* Adequate staff, assistance, budget.
* Friendship, support, positive people, harmonious relationships.

6) The trainer divides the participants into small groups (4-6 persons), or utilizes previously established discussion units. Participants are instructed to take 4-5 minutes each to show their picture to their group and summarize its meaning, sharing their assessment of the stressors and the energizers in their current work environment. (20-30 minutes).

Note: If participants are from the same company, they should be encouraged to share only as much as they feel is comfortable and prudent.

7) The trainer reconvenes the group and asks participants to help him construct a list of "Principles for Surviving in the Work World" that can be gleaned from this

exercise. The trainer records the major points on the blackboard/overhead as they emerge.

Issues that may be highlighted by the trainer if they are not described by the group include:

- Take the bad with the good -- every job has its rewards as well as its trials.

- Analyze your work setting -- not only from an efficiency point of view, but also in light of the energizers available for refueling.

- Set up a mutual admiration society-- everyone needs to be appreciated. If one person won't do it, find someone else. Compliment each other.

- Know what you can and what you cannot change -- some battles are worth fighting, others are not.

- Avoid all unnecessary meetings -- the number of meetings and the likelihood of burnout are positively correlated.

- Be a good bureaucrat -- the ability to influence is power. Play your cards wisely. Learn how to make a positive difference in the setting with whatever power you can muster.

- Experiment with revitalization -- no one strategy for surviving will work all the time. Be adventurous. Try something new for fun. Surprise someone!

VARIATION

- The length of this exercise can be shortened by dropping the embellishment process in Steps 4 and 5. Participants will still have great energy for, and find meaning in, sharing their symbolic pictures with each other.

TRAINER'S NOTES

46 LIFETRAP II: HOOKED ON HELPING

Participants affirm the admirable nature of their caring
for others and also examine the long-term stress and resulting exhaustion that is inevitable when care-giving becomes
an addiction. Although this extended, multi-process exercise is designed for "professional" helpers (nurses, counselors, clergy, teachers, etc), the issues apply to all caring
people -- especially working parents.

GOALS

1) To recognize, affirm and rejoice in care-giving commit-
    ments.

2) To examine the stress that results when people get
    hooked on caring for others first, regardless of the
    cost to self.

3) To explore options for controlling the care-givers'
    addiction while still reaching out in caring commit-
    ments to others.

GROUP SIZE

Unlimited

TIME FRAME

60-90 minutes

MATERIALS NEEDED

Blank paper, one copy of the "Hooked on Helping Addiction
Test" and "Hooked on Helping Beliefs" worksheets for each
participant.

PROCESS

Note: This is a five-part exercise:

    A) Introductory chalk talk on the care-giving addic-
       tion. (5-10 minutes)
    B) Guided reflection process exploring personal care-
       giving qualities. (15-20 minutes)
    C) Personal assessment using the Hooked on Helping
       Addiction Test and Beliefs Inventory (15-20 minutes)
    D) Small group sharing (20-30 minutes)
    E) Wrap-up with strategies for coping (5-10 minutes)

A) Care-Giving: A Stress-Producing Life Trap

1) The trainer introduces the subject of care-giving by
   soliciting from the group examples of the "helpful"
   things participants have done that day (eg, made lunch
   for my daughter, took the dog for a walk, drove a col-
   league to work, gave Mr James a backrub, bit back an
   angry retort, paid attention to my spouse, took an emergency call, cleaned up the bathroom, earned money for
   house payment, juggled work assignments, etc).

   *Note: If the group is not composed of "professional"
   care-givers who identify immediately with the
   issues raised here, the trainer may want to provide a more extensive warm-up to the topic. Ask
   "How many people here did something helpful today?"
   Solicit lots of examples. Then ask, "How many of
   you enjoy the process of doing something nice or
   caring for someone else?" Invite participants to
   describe how they feel when they've been helpful.*

2) After the group has generated a wide variety of helping
   behaviors, the trainer points out that all of us are
   care-givers -- sensitive, lively people who reach out
   to others and touch them. Unfortunately, this lifestyle can become a seductive life-trap that breeds
   stress. The trainer outlines the "Hooked on Helping"
   addiction process:

   ● We care-givers are admirable people. We usually
     have our antennae turned outwards toward others and
     whenever we pick up signals of need, we are prompted
     to respond, to reach out.

   ● Care-giving is extremely fulfilling. It's reward-
     ing to be sensitive, warm, loving and involved in
     others' lives. It also feels wonderful to be re-
     cognized as a special, caring, loving person.

   ● In fact, helping feels so satisfying that it's pos-
     sible to get hooked on the experience, becoming
     addicted to the payoffs of putting others' needs
     first. The admirable quality of caring for others
     also bears the risk of shortchanging ourselves.

   ● Hooked helpers know how to turn their compassion
     faucet "on" so their love flows out, but have for-
     gotten how to turn the faucet "off". Addicted
     care-givers are particularly vulnerable to stress
     exhaustion. When helpers spend months and even
     years carng for a parade of "others" without also
     caring for themselves, they may burn out -- and end
     up feeling empty and bitter.

● How do people get hooked on helping? We get hooked
   by our beliefs and life experience, starting at an
   early age. Many helpers come from families where
   caring for others was rewarded and "selfishness"
   was discouraged. Even though fulfilling all the
   family's wishes and demands would be impossible,
   "helper" children believe that they have the responsibility to take care of everyone else, regardless
   of their own feelings. Our beliefs keep us hooked
   on helping well into adulthood.

B) Examining the Care-Giver In You

3) The trainer distributes blank paper and invites partici-
    pants to get in touch with the wonderful, warm, gentle
    spirit of care-giving in themselves by reflecting on
    the following questions.

    *Note: This series of questions works best when partici-
          pants do not know the sequence ahead of time.
          Ask the questions one at a time, allowing ample
          opportunity for participants to answer each one
          thoughtfully before moving on.*

    □ Think of a person whom you would consider a model
      of caring and helpfulness -- a helpful hero or
      heroine, if you will. This person may be dead or
      alive, known to you personally or only by reputa-
      tion. Write down this person's name at the top of
      your page.

    □ In your mind consider this person. What is she
      like? How is she helpful? What are her qualities
      of caring that you admire most? Write them down.

    □ How are you like that person? Or in what ways
      would you like to emulate that person? Make note
      of these similarities and desired qualities.

    □ Think back to your earliest memories and make a note
      of the first time you can recall being "helpful".
      Perhaps it was when you washed the dishes for your
      mother, or defended a sibling, or assisted your
      first grade teacher. Jot down a few details about
      your first recollection of being "helpful".

    □ As you consider that early occasion, what were the
      qualities of helpfulness that you demonstrated in
      that instance? (eg, did work, gave encouragement,
      came to someone's defense, listened carefully, etc).

© 1984 Whole Person Press   PO Box 3151   Duluth MN 55803

❏ Think about yourself as a caring, helpful person. When you're at your very best -- what is it that you give to others?

❏ Think back to the time when you started your present profession (job/role/etc). What grand visions of caring and helping did you carry into your job when you started? (These dreams and visions may be very tender -- the kind of sensitive issues you usually don't talk about.) Write these visions down with all the excitement and grandiosity that you can recall feeling when you were fresh and idealistic.

❏ The ultimate helper's fantasy goes something like this: "I can . . . (a) work a miracle . . . (b) in a hopeless situation . . . (c) because I care so much." Few people ever really say this out loud, but most care-givers recognize the fantasy. There are countless variations, such as:

* Helping someone whom no one else could help -- by giving time or love . . .
* Single-handedly changing a bureaucratic system and being appreciated for it . . .
* Hoping you could take away someone's pain, by caring so much . . .

Write some detailed notes on your fantasy about how you can (a) work a miracle, (b) in a hopeless situation, (c) because you care so much.

❏ Look over all your answers and notice the rich variety of caring characteristics you've identified. Then write a paragraph describing yourself as if you possess every single caring quality you've identified (including those of your helpful hero/ heroine). Don't hedge by saying you're only this way some of the time. Write the paragraph as if you are all of these fine qualities all of the time. For example, you might write:

> I am sensitive, and when others are hurting I always listen and give them all the time that they need. I am loyal and trustworthy. People can depend on me to come through when they need me . . . etc . . . etc . . .

4) When participants have completed their paragraphs, the trainer asks them to form groups of four persons each. The trainer instructs participants to get acquainted by reading their paragraphs out loud to the group.

Participants are to <u>brag</u> wholeheartedly, introducing
themselves by describing all their helpful qualities in
full detail.

*Note: Participants will groan when you give this assign-
      ment. Don't worry. Simply laugh and tell them,
      "If you think God will get you for doing this,
      tell God -- 'the trainer up front made me do it!'"
      Instruct participants to refrain from any side
      comments that would undercut their bragging (eg,
      "Well, I'm not that way all the time, and some-
      times I'm also crabby", etc). Participants are
      to brag only, and feel how it feels!*

5) The trainer reconvenes the group and asks for reactions.
    Undoubtedly, reactions will be mixed -- "It was silly."
    "It felt good." "It was embarrassing." The trainer
    may point out the following concepts.

    ● Most people are "closet braggers" -- they want
      others to notice these good qualities but don't
      want others to notice that they're trying to get
      them to notice!

    ● The tender visions of caring and kindness we all
      carry in our hearts are powerful, positive motiva-
      tors, not to be denied or diminished, but to be
      relished and enjoyed!

    ● In one sense, stress exhaustion is a compliment!
      It "attacks" only those who care -- those who
      sparkle with enthusiasm for life. You have to have
      been on <u>FIRE</u> to burn out. Those who glow with en-
      thusiasm for people are the ones who experience the
      symptoms of burnout from caring -- too much!

C) <u>Exploring the Trap of Addiction</u>

    6) In order to help participants assess their own level of
        addiction to care-giving, the trainer distributes
        "Hooked on Helping Addiction Tests" to the group mem-
        bers and asks them to answer every question "yes" or
        "no", as honestly as they can.

    7) Participants total their "yes" responses and judge
        their addiction level according to the following scale
        as read by the trainer.

© 1984 Whole Person Press   PO Box 3151   Duluth MN 55803

0-1 = NOT ADDICTED

> People in this category may very well be
> excellent care-givers -- but they have
> learned how to include themselves on their
> care list as well.

2-4 = BORDERLINE ADDICTION

> The process of care-giving will at times ex-
> haust these folks to the point where they
> feel they "have no more to give." They will
> probably experience resulting symptoms of
> distress.

5-7 = ADDICTED CARE-GIVERS

> The unrestrained attempt to care for everyone
> all of the time leaves these people burned
> out and exhausted most of the time. These
> folks are trapped. Not knowing how to say
> "no" to others' needs, their only self-
> protection is to hide from others so they
> won't notice others' needs!

8) The trainer may ask for a show of hands to indicate the
range of scores in the group. She then asks the group
to share observations and insights. Some participants
may point out that their answers to the questions have
changed over the years as they have learned to take
better care of themselves.

9) The trainer points out the connection between personal
belief systems and the addiction to care-giving.

- The addiction to helping is the result of common,
well-intentioned but irrational personal beliefs
that lead to self-neglect.

- Before we can alter our lifestyle and come to grips
with our addiction, we need to modify the underly-
ing beliefs that guide our daily decisions.

10) The trainer distributes the "Hooked on Helping Beliefs"
worksheet and talks through the three care-giving syndromes. Participants mark for special attention the
irrational beliefs that are particularly troublesome to
them and complete the bottom portion of the worksheet.

D) <u>Small Group Sharing and Discussion</u> (20-30 minutes)

11) The trainer divides the participants into groups of
    four people each, or utilizes previously formed sharing
    groups. Participants take five minutes each to share
    personal insights generated by the "Hooked on Helping
    Addiction Test" and the "Beliefs" worksheets. Partici-
    pants may also describe stress-related symptoms they
    experience as a result of trying to be everything to
    others.

    *Note: The emphasis should be on personal sharing and
          listening, not advice-giving. Participants are
          to refrain from trying to "HELP" others. Rather
          they should simply listen as carefully as they
          can, and when their turn comes, share as person-
          ally as they are willing.*

12) The trainer reconvenes the total group and asks for a
    few general observations regarding the process.

E) <u>Unraveling the Trap of Addiction</u> (5-10 minutes)

13) Participants are asked -- as a total group -- to gener-
    ate a list of strategies for coping with the addiction
    to care-giving. If the group does not generate many,
    the trainer may wish to expand on some of the following
    ideas before closing the session.

    ● Individual irrational beliefs must be dislodged by
      countering them with more rational beliefs and ex-
      pectations. What are some "counters" to each of
      the "Hooked on Helping Beliefs"?

    ● Don't give up the dream of being a care-giver. It
      is this very dream that energizes us to reach out
      to others. Just don't expect to turn your dream
      into reality 100% of the time, or you'll soon be-
      come frustrated, down on yourself and emotionally
      exhausted.

    ● Keep others on your care-giving list, but learn to
      put your own name on the list as well. "Love your
      neighbor as yourself." If you don't care for your-
      self -- God help your neighbor! Neither of you
      will be cared for!

    ● Cultivate assertiveness skills. Saying "no" when
      you need to say "no" and "yes" when you need to say

"yes", and knowing the difference between the two,
is essential to recovery.

- If you're in a real pinch and you don't want to
  respond to someone else's need, admit that you're
  a member of "Helpers Anonymous". Say, "I'd like
  to -- but you see, I'm a recovering care-giver and
  I'm not allowed to right now!"

  *Note: HELPERS ANONYMOUS (p 65) makes a perfect
        finale to this exercise!*

VARIATIONS

- If time limitations prohibit the completion of this entire
  exercise, Sections B, C, and D can each be shortened or
  dropped. Each section can stand on its own with minor adap-
  tations. However, the depth of experience participants will
  gain from a limited version will be lessened accordingly.

- As an addendum to Section C, "Exploring The Trap of Addiction", the trainer may ask participants to complete the
  BURNOUT INDEX (p 24), or the STRESS SYMPTOM INVENTORY worksheet (Stress I, p 17). Participants would then be con-
  fronted by the draining results of the stress they impose
  upon themselves when trapped in the addiction to care-giving.

TRAINER'S NOTES

Adapted from Tubesing, Sippel and Loving Tubesing, R$_x$ For Burnout
(Duluth MN: Whole Person Press, 1981).

HOOKED ON HELPING ADDICTION TEST

Answer the seven questions below with a "yes" or "no". Try not
to hedge. Choose the answer that's more accurate for you right
now.

Yes No

☐   ☐   1) I will almost always listen to others who need emo-
            tional support, but I seldom ask anyone to pay
            attention to my emotional needs.

☐   ☐   2) When someone helps me I usually make sure I do as
            much or more to help them in return.

☐   ☐   3) When I don't respond to someone else's needs, I
            often feel selfish.

☐   ☐   4) I try hard not to hurt other people's feelings.

☐   ☐   5) Once I say "yes" people can count on me to get the
            job done, even if it costs me personally.

☐   ☐   6) I avoid conflict whenever possible.

☐   ☐   7) I tend to get myself in over my head by saying
            "yes" too much, too often.

___ ___ TOTALS
Yes No

HOOKED ON HELPING BELIEFS

Check yourself against these common care-giving syndromes. How
many of these assumptions do you act on? Be aware that rarely
do people actually speak these beliefs out loud. Mentally review your behaviors to find out whether you whisper any of these
messages to yourself.

The "SUPER-HELPER" Syndrome

_____ "I must be everything to everyone"
_____ "I must be able to help everyone"
_____ "I don't have the limits of normal people"

The "EMPTY POT" Syndrome

_____ "I must always try to help someone else if I'm asked"
_____ "Even though I feel empty, I can always find something
         more to give"
_____ "I must never be 'out to lunch'"

The "YOU FIRST" Syndrome

_____ "My needs aren't so important as yours"
_____ "It's selfish to take care of myself"
_____ "I'll get my needs met by helping you"

In what ways do these beliefs lead me into behaviors that cause
me distress?

_____

_____

_____

_____

_____

Observations and Comments

_____

_____

_____

47 CIRCUIT OVERLOAD

This assessment tool helps participants to see how much
stress they are currently "loading on the circuits".

GOALS

1) To generate a personal and group list of stressors.

2) To involve participants in a discussion of the under-
   lying causes of stress.

GROUP SIZE

Unlimited

TIME FRAME

15-20 minutes

MATERIALS NEEDED

"Circuit Overload" worksheets for all participants; blackboard or newsprint easel with markers.

PROCESS

1) The trainer introduces the exercise by describing how
   each of us is like a circuit box. When too many things
   go wrong, we overload the circuit, trip the breaker and
   lose our power.

2) The trainer distributes the "Circuit Overload" worksheets and asks participants individually to list all
   the things that currently cause them stress -- one in
   each of the circuit switches.

   *Note: The trainer may want to explain that this is not
          a race to see who can overload their circuits
          first -- although this might indicate one cause
          of stress! -- rather it is a tool to start the
          group thinking about stress in their lives.*

3) The trainer draws one large circuit box on the board.
   She asks for volunteers to share stressors, writing the
   responses on the large circuit box. When all the circuits are filled, the trainer invites participants to
   comment on the patterns they see in this list of stressors. Are they work-related? Family-oriented? In/out
   of your control? Do they involve relationships with
   others? Financial pressures?

VARIATION

- After Step 2, participants could pair up with a partner and compare lists, looking for common themes in their personal lists. Following this sharing, the trainer would reconvene the group and complete Step 3 of the exercise.

TRAINER'S NOTES

Submitted by Randy R Weigel

CIRCUIT OVERLOAD

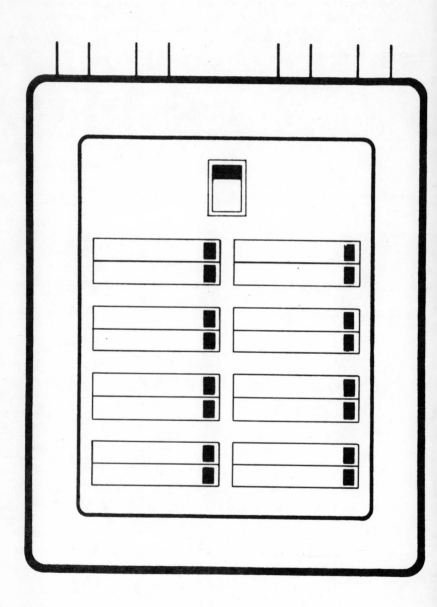

MANAGEMENT STRATEGIES

48 I'VE GOT RHYTHM (p 49)

This simple stress management strategy is based on the concept that there's a "right" time for everything. Participants identify the current rhythm of their lives and decide what plans will help them flow with, rather than fight against their natural rhythm.   (15-20 minutes)

49 PILEUP COPERS (p 54)

Using a unique deck of coping cards from the game "PILEUP" participants gain an overall view of possible coping options and identify their personal coping style, by sorting and discussing both the negative and positive coping cards.   (60 minutes)

50 MONTH OF FUNDAYS (p 61)

Participants explore the power of play as a stress management resource and make a plan for incorporating play into their lifestyle every day of the coming month.   (20-30 minutes)

51 THE WORRY STOPPER (p 64)

In this thought-provoking chalk talk and assessment, participants use the criteria of control and importance to determine what's worth worrying about.   (30-40 minutes)

52 CONSULTANTS UNLIMITED (p 70)

Participants act as a consultation team engaged to devise alternative stretegies for managing each others' "on-the-job" stressors.   (30-40 minutes)

48 I'VE GOT RHYTHM

This simple stress management strategy is based on the concept that there's a "right" time for everything. Participants identify the current rhythm of their lives and decide
what plans will help them flow with, rather than fight
against, their natural rhythm.

GOALS

1) To illustrate that in stress management, attention to
    personal timing issues is important.

2) To help participants identify and act upon their cur-
    rent personal life rhythms.

GROUP SIZE

Unlimited; also effective in work with individuals.

TIME FRAME

15-20 minutes

MATERIALS NEEDED

"My Current Rhythm" worksheet for each participants.

PROCESS

1) The trainer points out the relationship between personal
    rhythms and effective stress management by highlighting
    the following concepts:

    • Life consists of a variety of rhythms: regular
      heartbeats, periods of work and sleep, the days,
      the seasons and the tides. There is a time for
      everything: a time to mourn and a time to dance,
      a time to keep silent and a time to speak, a time
      to weep and a time to laugh, a time to work and a
      time to play.

    • Ancient cultures attended carefully to these pat-
      terns. Their sense of timing was highly developed.
      The Greeks even coined a word for the "right time."
      They called an opportune moment the "kairos".
      Earlier cultures have known that doing anything at
      the wrong time created inefficiency and, at times,
      disaster.

- Unfortunately, in our culture most of that wisdom
  has been lost. Most people are out of touch with
  their natural rhythm. Awakened by alarm clocks,
  eating lunch when their supervisor tells them to,
  hurrying to finish school, visiting Mother on Sunday
  afternoon, their natural rhythm is interrupted.

- Resisting one's natural rhythm and sense of timing
  takes a lot more energy than going with its cadence.
  Continuously swimming against the flow of your
  life's current rather than floating with it creates
  excess stress.

2) Using the script below, the trainer asks participants to
   get in touch with their own personal rhythm.

> Please stand up. Try for a moment to become aware
> of your own rhythm. Start moving in some way (walk-
> ing, swaying, stretching, bouncing, bending) until
> you find a style and pace that feels natural, com-
> fortable, familiar. Really tune in to yourself. Do
> what feels good. Pay attention to your heartbeat,
> your breathing, your muscle tone, your sense of
> balance. (2 minutes)
>
> Now, speed up your movement a little bit, then more
> dramatically. Be aware of how this hurried pace
> feels. (1 minute)
>
> Return to your natural rhythm now. See how that
> feels in comparison. (1 minute)
>
> Now slow your pace way down. Be aware of how this
> slowdown affects your breathing, your balance, your
> heartbeat. (1 minute)

The trainer invites comments from the group on what they
experienced in relation to their internal rhythm.

3) Participants complete the "My Current Rhythm" worksheet.
   They are to jot down the first response that comes to
   mind.

4) The trainer makes the following suggestion for adjust-
   ing stress management plans to fit with the sense of
   rhythm and personal timing.

- Pay attention to your personal rhythm. Let your
  rhythm guide your actions. Trust your internal
  wisdom. Attend to your own needs of the moment.
  If now is a time to be quiet, be quiet. If it's

time for you to fight, then fight.   If it's a
time to play, play wholeheartedly.   You can't make
jam 'til the strawberries are picked.

- If you're a "charger," always going full bore and
  forcing yourself to accomplish too much too quickly,
  then your task is to learn to throttle back to your
  natural rhythm rather than scrambling to stay ahead
  of yourself.   Your challenge is to listen to the
  subtle sounds of life within you and swing along
  with the cadence of that music.   If you're worried
  about missing the boat, remember the Titanic.

- If you're a "lagger" who crawls along, hanging back
  and procrastinating, then you, too, need to listen.
  There are "right" moments for bold and daring actions.   Seize them and go for it.

- Conserve your energy.   Just ride along through the
  jolts and delays of life, instead of fighting them.
  Why not?   Your rhythm will carry you.

VARIATIONS

- This process can be utilized as a warm-up preceeding an in-
  depth planning exercise.   Participants are urged to take
  their current life rhythms seriously as they construct
  their personal plans for change.

- As part of Step 3, participants could share insights with
  each other in their pre-existing small groups or form new
  groups to discuss "current rhythms."

TRAINER'S NOTES

Adapted from the Stress Skills Participant Workbook (Duluth MN:
Whole Person Press, 1977) and Kicking Your Stress Habits (Duluth
MN: Whole Person Press, 1981).

MY CURRENT RHYTHM

1) How do you normally respond to the rhythm of your life?

   ☐ I'm usually pushing ahead of my own rhythm.
   ☐ I'm usually right in harmony with my own rhythm.
   ☐ I'm usually lagging behind my natural rhythm.

   At this moment I'm _____ the rhythm of my life.
                     (ahead of/behind/right in step with)

2) Use these questions to help identify your natural rhythm at this particular
   time in your life. Write down the first thought that enters your mind.

   Maybe I don't need to be/do _____ any more.
                               (something you need to give up)

   Maybe I still need to be/do _____ some more.
                               (something you need to hang on to)

   Maybe I need to be/do _____ sometime soon.
                         (a future direction or goal)

   Maybe I need to be/do _____ once again.
                         (a past resource or strength to revive)

   Maybe I need to be/do _____ sometimes.
                         (something inconsistent or tentative)

Now is the "right time" for you! But what is it the right time for? Look at your answers so far. What is the "kairos" for you right now?

Now is the right time for me to _____

_____

_____

3) Take your insights seriously as you create a plan for stress management.

Based on my current rhythm, these are some elements I should/should not include in my stress management plan:

I should include _____   I should not include _____

_____   _____

_____   _____

_____

4) *Please note: Each time you respond to these questions, your answers will probably be different. Why not? Your rhythm is constantly in flux. Answer these questions again on the 12th day of each month. Then post your answers on the refrigerator door!*

49 PILEUP COPERS

Using a unique deck of coping cards from the game "PILEUP" participants gain an overall view of possible coping options and identify their personal coping style, by sorting and discussing both the negative and positive coping cards.

GOALS

1) To illustrate the difference between positive and negative copers.

2) To explore the full range of coping options.

3) To assess personal coping patterns.

GROUP SIZE

Unlimited; also works extremely well in work with individuals and/or family units.

TIME FRAME

60 minutes

MATERIALS NEEDED

One deck of "PILEUP" cards for every four participants (available from Whole Person Press); tables for use in sorting and piling cards.

PROCESS

Note: This exercise is most effective when each participant can sort the cards. However, if the trainer is not able to obtain an ample number of PILEUP decks, the exercise can be adapted. Make your own cards or present the copers in a worksheet format.

1) The trainer introduces the subject of coping with the following concepts:

   ● Most people cope successfully with 98% of their stressors. We make hundreds of adjustments each day, and manage most situations quite well.

   ● Usually no single strategy will be effective in managing all of life's challenges. That's why we need a variety of coping skills.

- Most people use three or four favorite coping
  styles over and over again -- copers they rely on
  regularly to get through most tough situations.

2) The trainer instructs participants to think of their
   three or four favorite, tried and true stress remedies
   -- the ways they cope by habit. Participants then
   share a few examples with the group.

3) The trainer divides participants into groups of four
   persons each, and encourages each group to find adequate
   table space for working together. The trainer then distributes one deck of PILEUP cards to each group. Group
   members divide the cards by color, keeping the red cards
   (negative copers) and green cards (positive copers) and
   setting the yellow cards (stressors) and rainbow cards
   (creative) aside.

4) The trainer introduces the subject of negative coping
   with the following remarks.

   Every one of your coping mechanisms works -- or you
   wouldn't use it again! But some copers have a high
   cost. We call these negative copers. Smoking, eating,
   and drinking do bring immediate relief from tension --
   but the positive effects don't last long and the negative side effects are often quite serious.

   Most negative copers are effective short-term stress
   relievers, but they create additional problems if
   repeated over a long period of time or in response to
   many stressors.

5) Participants are instructed to lay out all the negative
   (red) coping cards on the table and to look them over
   carefully. The trainer then asks each participant to
   select the card representing a negative coper he is
   likely to use when under great stress.

   Each participant identifies his negative coper and
   shares with the group 1) what this coper does for him,
   and 2) what it "costs" him when he uses it.

6) The trainer then introduces the concept of positive
   copers -- those techniques that are reliable stress
   relievers without the negative side effects. These
   skills can be used over and over again for a variety
   of stressful situations.

   The trainer describes the six major coping strategies
   represented as "suits" in the PILEUP cards -- physical,

emotional, mental, interpersonal, family and diversions
-- and the six skills included in each suit.

*Note: The six suits of positive copers (36 skills in
all) are outlined below. Be sure to point out the
symbol used for each category on the PILEUP cards.*

7) The trainer instructs group members to each take a turn
   sorting the positive copers (green cards) into piles
   that seem relevant to them. The person sorting talks
   through her decision-making process while she sorts.
   After all the cards are placed in piles, she looks
   through each stack and shares her insights and observations about her coping pattern. Then the next person
   takes his turn, using his own categories for sorting.

   *Note: The trainer may want to give examples of possible
   categories (eg, "give myself a grade - A,B,C,D,F"
   or "use frequently, use sometimes, never use" or
   "appropriate/not appropriate for my current stress.
   But the exercise is most rewarding when people make
   up their own criteria.*

8) The trainer raises a few final questions for participants to consider in the small groups.

   □ Are your commonly-used copers clustered in one
     category or coping suit? Or are they well distri-
     buted throughout the suits?

   □ Which one or two copers that you don't use now
     might be the most effective additions to your
     repertoire of coping skills?

   □ How might you practice these new copers? In what
     situations might you use them? Against what
     stressor(s)?

9) The trainer reconvenes the group, collects the cards
   and asks participants to share their insights and
   observations.

*Note: The colorful PILEUP cards with instructions for 12 addi-
tional games are available for $15.95 from Whole Person
Press. Quantity discounts available on card decks for use
in this exercise. Write or call for a quotation!*

*The PILEUP cards were originally developed by Whole Person
Associates as part of THE STRESS KIT © Aid Association for
Lutherans, 1982.*

NEGATIVE COPERS**

ALCOHOL: Drink to change your mood.
             Use alcohol as your friend.

DENIAL: Pretend nothing's wrong.
             Lie. Ignore the problem.

DRUGS: Abuse coffee/aspirin/medications.
            Smoke pot. Pop pills.

EATING: Keep binging. Go on a diet.
             Use food to console you.

FAULT-FINDING: Have a judgmental attitude.
                    Complain. Criticize.

ILLNESS: Develop headaches/nervous stomach/major illness.
              Become accident prone.

INDULGING: Stay up late. Sleep in.
                Buy on impulse. Waste time.

PASSIVITY: Hope it gets better. Procrastinate.
                Wait for a lucky break.

REVENGE: Get even. Be sarcastic.
              Talk mean.

STUBBORNNESS: Be rigid. Demand your way.
                   Refuse to be wrong.

TANTRUMS: Yell. Mope. Pout. Swear.
               Drive recklessly.

TOBACCO: Smoke to relieve tension.
              Smoke to be "in".

WITHDRAWAL: Avoid the situation. Skip school or work.
                 Keep your feelings to yourself.

WORRYING: Fret over things.
               Imagine the worst.

**From the PILEUP card game, © 1982 Aid Association for Lutherans.

POSITIVE COPERS**

DIVERSIONS

GETAWAYS :	Spend time alone. See a movie. Daydream.
HOBBIES :	Write. Paint. Remodel. Create something.
LEARNING :	Take a class. Read. Join a club.
MUSIC :	Play an instrument. Sing. Listen to the stereo.
PLAY :	Play a game. Go out with friends.
WORK :	Tackle a new project. Keep busy. Volunteer.

FAMILY

BALANCING :	Balance time at work and home. Accept the good with the bad.
CONFLICT RESOLUTION :	Look for win/win solutions. Forgive readily.
ESTEEM-BUILDING :	Build good family feelings. Focus on personal strengths.
FLEXIBILITY :	Take on new family roles. Stay open to change.
NETWORKING :	Develop friendships with other families. Make use of community resources.
TOGETHERNESS :	Take time to be together. Build family traditions. Express affection.

INTERPERSONAL

AFFIRMATION :	Believe in yourself. Trust others. Give compliments.
ASSERTIVENESS :	State your needs and wants. Say "no" respectfully.
CONTACT :	Make new friends. Touch. Really listen to others.
EXPRESSION :	Show feelings. Share feelings.
LIMITS :	Accept others' boundaries. Drop some involvements.
LINKING :	Share problems with others. Ask for support from family/friends.

**From the PILEUP card game, © 1982 Aid Association for Lutherans.

POSITIVE COPERS**

MENTAL

IMAGINATION :	Look for the humor. Anticipate the future.
LIFE PLANNING :	Set clear goals. Plan for the future.
ORGANIZING :	Take charge. Make order. Don't let things pile up.
PROBLEM-SOLVING :	Solve it yourself. Seek outside help. Tackle problems head-on.
RELABELING :	Change perspectives. Look for good in a bad situation.
TIME MANAGEMENT :	Focus on top priorities. Work smarter, not harder.

PHYSICAL

BIOFEEDBACK :	Listen to your body. Know your physical limitations.
EXERCISE :	Pursue physical fitness. Jog. Swim. Dance. Walk.
NOURISHMENT :	Eat for health. Limit use of alcohol.
RELAXATION :	Tense and relax each muscle. Take a warm bath. Breathe deeply.
SELF-CARE :	Energize your work and play. Strive for self-improvement.
STRETCHING :	Take short stretch breaks throughout your day.

SPIRITUAL

COMMITMENT :	Take up a worthy cause. Say "yes". Invest yourself meaningfully.
FAITH :	Find purpose and meaning. Trust God.
PRAYER :	Confess. Ask forgiveness. Pray for others. Give thanks.
SURRENDER :	Let go of problems. Learn to live with the situation.
VALUING :	Set priorities. Be consistent. Spend time and energy wisely.
WORSHIP :	Share beliefs with others. Put faith into action.

**From the PILEUP card game, © 1982 Aid Association for Lutherans.

TRAINER'S NOTES

© 1984   Whole Person Press   PO Box 3151   Duluth MN 55803

50 MONTH OF FUNDAYS

Participants explore the power of play as a stress management strategy and make a plan for incorporating play into
their lifestyle every day of the coming month.

GOALS

1) To promote playfulness as a stress management technique.

2) To build play into each day's schedule for one month.

GROUP SIZE

Unlimited

TIME FRAME

20-30 minutes

MATERIALS NEEDED

"Month of Fundays" worksheet for all participants.

PROCESS

*Note: The GARDEN parable (p 113) makes a good introduction
or closing for this exercise.*

1) The trainer introduces the exercise with a few brief
comments on the importance of play as a stress management strategy.

- People often get tense because they focus so much
on logic, order, production, etc. Play is meaning-
less activity that we do just because it feels good!
Play allows us an opportunity to indulge our creative, intuitive right brain functions.

- Play helps us blow off steam and relax in body, mind
and spirit. It also helps us maintain some of our
child-like wonder and care-lessness.

- Play is a form of re-creation that provides a
healthy counter balance to work. All of us are en-
titled to guilt-free play time.

- All work and no play makes Jack or Jill a nervous
wreck!

© 1984 Whole Person Press   PO Box 3151   Duluth MN 55803

2) The trainer asks participants to list 5-10 "playful"
    activities they engage in regularly or occasionally
    (eg, surfing, sex, tickling sprees, trips to an amuse-
    ment park, practical jokes, etc).

    Next, they are invited to recall the wide variety of
    activities they did for "fun" during childhood or ado-
    lescense (flying kites, magic tricks, rolling in the
    leaves, digging in the mud, riding bikes, throwing
    stones, kick the can, wrestling, paper dolls, roller
    skating). Participants list 15-20 different ways they
    used to play.

3) As an experiment in stress management, the trainer
    challenges participants to commit themselves to playing
    for at least 15 minutes each day during the next month.
    The "Month of Fundays Calendars" are distributed. Par-
    ticipants fill in the calendar, choosing one playful
    activity for each day from the lists they generated
    earlier.

    *Note: Encourage people to ask their neighbors for sug-
           gestions if they get stuck. It's okay to plan
           the same play activity more than once!*

4) The trainer invites everyone to join in a playful clos-
    ing activity (eg, a "Hokey Pokey" dance, a rousing
    chorus of "Boom, Boom, Ain't It Great To Be Crazy!",
    musical chairs, or a giant game of tag).

    *Note: MINE-HA-HA (Stress I, p 84); PULLING STRINGS
           (Stress I, p 124); or MUSICAL MOVEMENT (p 120)
           would work well.*

VARIATION

● Invite a number of children to the session as a "panel of
  experts" on play. Let the kids teach the adults how to
  play and let them suggest activities for the "Month of
  Fundays" calendar.

TRAINER'S NOTES

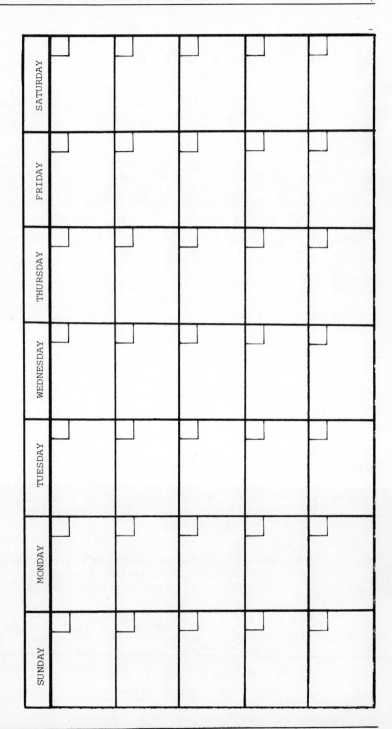

MONTH OF FUNDAYS

SUNDAY	MONDAY	TUESDAY	WEDNESDAY	THURSDAY	FRIDAY	SATURDAY

51 THE WORRY STOPPER

In this thought-provoking chalk talk and assessment, participants use the criteria of <u>control</u> and <u>importance</u> to determine what's worth worrying about.

GOALS

1) To explore the multitudes of things people worry about
    -- both the trivial and the important.

2) To underline the importance of values in effective
    stress management.

3) To provide a tool for deciding what's worth worrying
    about.

GROUP SIZE

Unlimited; with a large group the trainer will need a
movable microphone with a cord long enough to reach into
the audience.

TIME FRAME

30-40 minutes

MATERIALS NEEDED

"My Worry List" and "The Worry Stopper" worksheets for all
participants.

PROCESS

1) The trainer introduces the exercise by asking the group
    for a show of hands in response to the questions:
    ☐ How many people never worry?
    ☐ Who here is an expert on worrying?

2) The trainer moves out into the audience with a micro-
    phone (Donahue style) and asks some of the expert
    worriers what, specifically, they worry about.

    *Note: Stay with one person until he "runs dry!" You may
    need to prime the pump periodically with leading
    questions like, "What are you worrying about right
    now?" "What does your spouse worry about?" "Your
    kids?" "Your parents?" The idea is to generate
    a wide range of worries -- both trivial and
    profound -- from each person.*

3) After 5 or 6 people have shared their worries, the trainer distributes the "Worry List" worksheets to everyone and challenges them to write down everything they worry about, using the prompting questions on the worksheet to help trigger their awareness.

   Note: The trainer may want to elaborate, giving more examples of the kinds of things people might worry about (eg, "Does my breath smell?" "Did I unplug the coffee pot?" "Is my son using drugs?" "Am I pregnant?" "Did the gas bill come?" "Will I be able to afford a new coat?" "Will my tires last the winter?" "Will there be a drought this year?" "Will I have any cavities?" "Will I get stuck in the elevator?" "Will Social Security be bankrupt when I get there?" "Can I lose 10 pounds by summer?", etc).

4) The trainer comments that there seem to be lots of worrying experts here after all! She goes on to make some general observations about worry and stress, covering some or all of the points outlined below:

   • Most people are astounded at the number of life situations they are worried about at a given moment in time. Usually these worries lurk at the edges of our awareness until some stimulus brings one or more into focus.

   • Worrying is a useless waste of energy unless it motivates us to take some action to deal with the perceived threat.

   • Some experts estimate that up to 95% of our stress reactions are in response to the trivial rather than the important events in life. This process results from faulty perceptions and murky values that lead us to worry unnecessarily.

   • Rather than deciding clearly what's worth worrying about, we all too often end up in the same boat with the anonymous worrier who penned these lines:
       "It's the little things that bother
       and keep you on the rack,
       You can sit upon a mountain
       but not upon a tack!"

   • Some recent studies suggest that the distinction between eustress and distress may be primarily determined by our perception of control. If we feel in control, even an extremely anxiety-provoking situation may be seen as challenging rather than

distressful. If we feel powerless, even the most
trivial worry can be distressing.

- The key to effective stress management is to worry
  wisely -- to spend our energy on the things we
  truly value and those we can control.

5) The trainer distributes the "Worry Stopper" worksheets
and invites participants to diagnose their own worry
patterns. She instructs everyone to look over his worry
list and transfer each item to the appropriate panel of
the Worry Stopper based on his answers to the questions:
  □ Is this really important to me?
  □ Is this in my control?

Worries that are important and in his control are trans-
ferred to Panel I of the Worry Stopper. Worries that
are important but not in his control are written in
Panel II. Panel III is for worries that are not important and not in his control. Worries that are in his
control but are not important are placed in Panel IV.

6) The trainer asks participants to examine their entries
in each panel and at the bottom of the worksheet jot
down whatever general comments strike them about the
panel and the worries it contains.

7) The trainer reviews the panels one at a time, soliciting
input from the group as she reviews appropriate coping
strategies for each.

- Panel I - Since these items are important to us and
  also in our control, they are certainly worth worrying about -- especially if our concern motivates
  us to get moving on needed change. However, if
  this panel is filled to overflowing, we may need to
  reconsider how important each of these items really
  is. Relabeling skills might help us move some of
  these worries into Panel IV.

- Panel II - Since these items are important, but not
  in our control, we either need to gain some control
  and move the worry to Panel I or use our surrender
  skills. If we truly cannot change the situation,
  we need to let go!

- Panel III - It's surprising how many life situations
  we worry about that are neither in our control nor
  really important to us. Why waste an ounce of our
  precious energy on these items? Why not cross them
  off the worry list right now!

- <u>Panel IV</u> - If the items in this panel are not really important to us, we need to ask ourselves whether they are worth fretting about. It's amazing how much time and energy we spend working on trivia just because we can control it. Why worry about or try to change something that's not really important?

8) The trainer helps participants generate their personal "worry stopper" plan. She directs everyone to circle one item in each panel that he wants to stop worrying about. For each choice he writes a brief description of how he will accomplish the goal (eg, "I'm going to go have this lump checked." "Everytime the thought of rising taxes crosses my mind, I'll say 'let the governor worry about it!'" "Instead of worrying about whether my spouse is an alcoholic, I'll start going to Alanon." etc). As many participants as choose to are encouraged to stand up and read one or more of their worry-stopping resolutions.

Note: The trainer may want to close this exercise with the TREASURE CHEST FANTASY (p 132) or one of the skill-builders from I SURRENDER! (Stress I, p 78).

TRAINER'S NOTES

We learned this technique from Fay Zachary at the First Annual Conference on Burnout in Philadelphia.

© 1984   Whole Person Press   PO Box 3151   Duluth MN 55803

MY WORRY LIST

List everything you worry about -- big things, little things, anything that causes you concern or makes you uneasy. Be sure to include worries about:
  * Personal health and well-being, comfort, success, safety, behavior.
  * Immediate and extended family, health, finances, changes.
  * Job-related concerns, people, performance, future.
  * Neighborhood and community issues, taxes, politics, schools.
  * Ultimate life questions.
  * Global issues, war, natural resources, human rights.
  * Trivia, the little things that bother.

© 1984   Whole Person Press   PO Box 3151   Duluth MN 55803

THE WORRY STOPPER

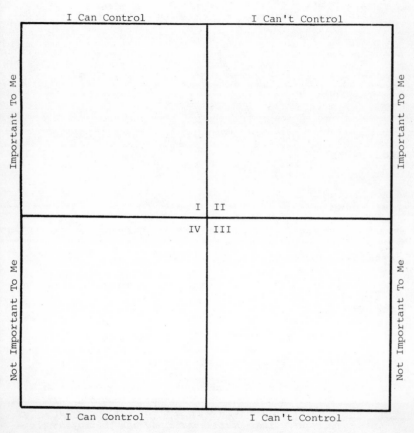

OBSERVATIONS:

    Panel I

    Panel II

    Panel III

    Panel IV

52 CONSULTANTS UNLIMITED

Participants act as a consultation team engaged to devise alternative strategies for managing each others' "on-the-job" stressors.

GOALS

1) To generate and evaluate coping strategies for specific job stressors.

2) To reinforce the concept of peer consultation as a problem-solving model.

GROUP SIZE

10-30

TIME FRAME

5-10 minutes for each consultation; 30-45 minutes in all.

MATERIALS NEEDED

One or more 3" x 5" index cards for each person; newsprint.

PROCESS

1) The trainer distributes 3" x 5" cards to participants and asks everyone to describe briefly on the card one source of stress in their work setting.

   Note: The trainer needs to reassure the group that all stress "entries" will remain anonymous. If people in the group know each other well, suggest a few guidelines participants may use to protect themselves and others in their work setting:

   * *Phrase your stressor in general terms.*
   * *Do not use names.*
   * *Keep the focus on how you experience the stress rather than blaming, judging or complaining.*

   If the group is small (less than 15 people), encourage participants to submit 2 or 3 stressors so the pool is larger and more anonymous.

2) The trainer collects the stressor cards, selects one (either at random or because it is "typical") and reads

it to the group; she invites everyone to join the consultation team by imagining alternative ways to deal with
the stress. The group brainstorms strategies that might
be helpful in coping with that specific job situation.
Each suggestion is recorded on the newsprint. (3 minutes)

3) The group is asked to decide on the three best strategies
among those listed. (2 minutes)

*Note: The point here is to identify several workable
coping plans. There is no magic in choosing
three -- two or four will do fine.*

4) The trainer chooses another job stressor for consultation. Steps 2 and 3 are repeated using a clean newsprint to record management alternatives for this
stressor.

5) The group continues to consult using this model until
their energy flags or suggestions get repetitive. The
trainer invites participants to comment on their insights and learnings from this process.

*Note: At the end of the session, participants may want
to claim the brainstorm newsprint referring to
their job situation.*

VARIATION

■ Participants could be divided into 3 or 4 person consultation teams who brainstorm strategies for dealing with each
others' stressful job situations.

TRAINER'S NOTES

TRAINER'S NOTES

SKILL BUILDERS

53 ATTITUDE ADJUSTMENT HOUR (p 73)

In this lively exercise participants practice the art of altering their viewpoint by telling and retelling the stories of their day from different perspectives. (25-35 minutes)

54 SPEAK UP! (p 77)

Participants explore the value of assertiveness as a coping skill by pairing up and experimenting with alternative styles both for making requests and for saying "no." (40-45 minutes)

55 AFFIRMATIVE ACTION PLAN (p 81)

In this attitude-changing exercise participants draw up a plan for using affirmation to manage a workplace stressor.
(40-50 minutes)

56 ANCHORING (p 88)

Participants guide one another through a relaxation fantasy and "anchor" the comfortable feelings they experience for later recall and stimulation of the relaxation response. (30 minutes)

57 THE ABC'S OF TIME (p 92)

This skill-building exercise illustrates the importance of spending time where it counts. Participants list the activities and tasks that consumed yesterday's 24 hours, then assess whether or not they invested effort in their top priorities. (40-50 minutes)

53 ATTITUDE ADJUSTMENT HOUR

In this lively exercise participants practice the art of
altering their viewpoint by telling and retelling the
stories of their day from different perspectives.

GOALS

1) To demonstrate the role of perception in the management
    of stress.

2) To help participants practice making conscious shifts
    in their perceptual patterns.

GROUP SIZE

Unlimited; also works well in family counseling.

TIME FRAME

25-35 minutes

MATERIALS NEEDED

"Accident Reports"

PROCESS

1) The trainer emphasizes the role of perception in both
    the creation of stress and its successful management,
    by outlining the following concepts:

    • Any life event, major or minor, can become a cause
       of stress if we view it as a threat. Stress is our
       reaction to whatever dangers we see around us. Per-
       ception is the key to stress management. Our stress
       level is determined by the way we label events
       (perception). If we see "safety" we remain relaxed.
       If we see "danger" we fight back with stress.

    • Incredible as it sounds, most of our stress comes
       from between our ears. If we don't like it, we can
       get rid of it, by changing our mind.

    • It's no more phoney to be "Pollyanna-ish" (seeing
       the rosy side of very tough problems) than it is to
       be cynical (seeing the negative side of positive
       opportunities).

    • At any given moment, we always have numerous

perceptual options available to us -- many ways to
view our situations. Our choices of viewpoints,
to a large extent, color the quality and feeling
tone of our daily experiences.

- In our society "attitude adjustment hour" is synony-
  mous with drinking alcohol. Yes, alcohol does alter
  people's mood. But true attitude adjustment comes
  only from making the choice to change our perception. This exercise offers an opportunity for you
  to practice the skill of seeing your life from many
  different possible viewpoints.

2) The trainer directs participants to find partners. Each
   person in the dyad takes two minutes to describe her
   day to her partner. (4 minutes total)

   *Note: If this exercise is being used early in the day,
         ask participants to describe yesterday.*

3) The trainer tells participants that in a few moments
   they will be challenged to "adjust their attitudes" and
   re-describe their days using a different viewpoint. He
   outlines the eight alternate perspectives they could
   potentially use, writing each suggestion on the board
   as it is described:

Re-tell the story of your day <u>AS IF</u> it were . . .

* A SITUATION COMEDY -- a big joke and the joke is on
                            you.
* A GREEK TRAGEDY -- as if you were meant to suffer and
                       you surely did.
* A SOAP OPERA -- of heroic proportions, with all the
                    subtlety, intrigue and drama of the
                    tube.
* A FAIRYTALE -- perfectly positive and enjoyable,
                   everything rosy.
* A BORE -- no expressions, dull, ho-hum, nothing much
              interesting.
* AN ATHLETIC CONTEST -- using sports metaphors as you
                           "drive for the goal", "take a
                           time out", "strike out", "hit
                           an ace", etc.
* A PITIFUL MESS -- you're lousy and you mess every-
                      thing up, and your life stinks.
* A TRAP -- everyone's out to get you and you have a
              lot to complain about.

*Note: This is a good time to read a sampling of the
       "Accident Reports" statements. The laughter gen-
       erated by these absurd attitude adjustments should
       stimulate the group's creativity.*

© 1984 Whole Person Press   PO Box 3151   Duluth MN 55803

4)   The trainer instructs the older person in each pair to
     choose one of the altered perspectives and re-describe
     her day to her partner using that viewpoint. (2 minutes)

     *Note: Encourage participants to be as dramatic as pos-
            sible in their descriptions and to really "get
            into" the chosen viewpoint.*

     The younger partner chooses a <u>different</u> viewpoint, ad-
     justs his attitude, and re-tells the story of his day
     from this new perspective. (2 minutes)

5)   Step 4 is repeated two or three times, allowing both
     partners an opportunity to re-view their day from
     several perspectives.

6)   The trainer reconvenes the group. Participants are
     asked to consider and comment on the following questions:

     □ How did the changed viewpoint alter your feelings?

     □ How do you normally choose to tell your day's story?

     □ What difference would it make in your life if you
       regularly sat down at the end of the day for an
       "attitude adjustment hour" in which you told and
       retold your day's story from different perspectives?

     □ How can you incorporate the principles of percep-
       tion into your day right while it's happening?

VARIATION

■ Instead of instructing participants to retell their day
  "as if it were . . .", the trainer may suggest that participants retell their day from someone else's perspective.
  (2 minutes each)

     "How would your day be described by . . ."
     * Your boss/supervisor/subordinate?
     * Your spouse?
     * Your kids/parents?
     * An investigative reporter from TV news?
     * A neighbor?
     * People you serve (clients, customers, parishoners)?

TRAINER'S NOTES

© 1984 Whole Person Press   PO Box 3151   Duluth MN 55803

ACCIDENT REPORTS*

- *Coming home, I drove into the wrong house and collided with a tree I didn't have.*

- *The other car collided with mine without even giving warning of its intentions.*

- *I collided with a stationary truck coming the other way.*

- *A truck backed through my windshield into my wife's face.*

- *A pedestrian hit me and went under my car.*

- *The guy was all over the road. I had to swerve a number of times before I hit him.*

- *I pulled away from the side of the road, glanced at my mother-in-law, and headed for the embankment.*

- *As I approached the intersection a sign suddenly appeared in a place where no sign had ever appeared before. I was unable to stop in time to avoid the accident.*

- *To avoid hitting the car in front of me, I struck the pedestrian.*

- *In my attempt to hit a fly, I drove into a telephone pole.*

- *My car was legally parked and it backed into the other vehicle.*

- *I told the police that I was not injured, but upon removing my hat, I found that I had a fractured skull.*

- *The pedestrian had no idea which direction to run, so I ran over him.*

- *The indirect cause of this accident was a little guy in a small car with a big mouth.*

- *An invisible car came out of nowhere, struck my vehicle and vanished.*

- *I had been driving for forty years when I fell asleep at the wheel.*

- *I saw a sad-faced old gentleman as he glanced off of the hood of my car.*

- *I was thrown from my car as it left the road. I was later found in a ditch by some stray cows.*

- *The telephone pole was approaching; I was attempting to swerve out of the way when it struck my front end.*

- *I was on my way to the doctor with rear end trouble when my universal joint gave way causing me to have an accident.*

*Each of these is an actual statement gleaned from official accident reports submitted to police and insurance investigators.

54 SPEAK UP!

Participants explore the value of assertiveness as a coping
skill by pairing up and experimenting with alternative
styles both for making requests and for saying "no".

GOALS

1) To assess personal comfort and skill in asking for
   things and in saying "no".

2) To learn the difference between effective and ineffec-
   tive requests and refusals.

3) To practice assertive direct expression of requests and
   refusals.

GROUP SIZE

Unlimited

TIME FRAME

40-45 minutes

MATERIALS NEEDED

Newsprint easel or blackboard.

PROCESS

1) The trainer introduces the general concepts of assertiveness and underlines the importance of assertiveness
   as a coping skill.

   ● It's amazing how much stress we could eliminate
     from our lives by practicing two simple techniques
     -- saying "no" (to unrewarding activities, extra
     obligations, inappropriate requests, etc), and
     asking directly for what we want. Making direct
     requests of others and turning down requests from
     others are two components of assertive behavior.

   ● Most of us stress ourselves and the people around
     us with our style of making requests and of giving
     responses to other's requests. All too often,
     people are either so passive that others have to
     guess at their meaning, or so aggressive that
     others feel the sting of their anger. Neither the
     non-assertive nor the aggressive pattern is a very
     effective style of communicating.

- Non-assertive people have difficulty asking for
  things directly, They tend to either avoid asking,
  or they ask in such an indirect, self-effacing way
  that their requests are often not understood, or
  are easily turned down. Likewise, when they say
  "no", they tend to be indirect and give excuses instead of stating the real reasons for their hesi-
  tation. Non-assertive people are also easily per-
  suaded to do what they don't want to do. These non-
  assertive behaviors are a sure-fire source of stress
  for both the requester and the responder.

- Aggressive people tend to be the opposite. They
  will make requests willingly and say "no" clearly,
  but do so in a manner that tends to be coercive,
  hostile, demanding and disrespectful. Such behavior
  is also often stressful to both giver and receiver.

2) The trainer asks participants to give examples of both
    non-assertive and aggressive ways to make and refuse
    requests.

    *Note: The trainer may want to role play several examples
          for the class.*

          The book How To Make Yourself Miserable *by Dan
          Greenberg includes some wonderful cynical dia-
          logues demonstrating how to make sure your request
          is rejected. These amusing vignettes could be
          read by the trainer to add humor, since they are
          guaranteed to solicit empathic chuckles from the
          group.*

3) The trainer asks participants to recall and note a
    recent stressful incident when someone requested some-
    thing from them and they had difficulty saying "no."

    Participants are asked to remember and note another
    recent experience when they felt under stress about
    asking for something they wanted.

4) Making a reasonable request; saying "no". The trainer
    asks group members to form pairs. Each pair decides
    who will be the "asker" and who will be the "refuser."

    The "asker" is instructed to think of a series of reason-
    able requests that she can make of the other person
    (eg, "I'd like a hug" or "Tell me what you think of me"
    or "Could I borrow a quarter for the phone", etc). The
    "refuser" is directed to respond with one word only: "no".
    When everyone understands the instructions clearly, the
    trainer tells the pairs to begin the request and refusal

---

process, keeping it up for three minutes. At the end
of that time, the pairs reverse roles and repeat this
activity for another three minutes. (6 minutes)

5) While allowing people to stay with their partners, the
    trainer solicits a brief discussion from the entire
    group concerning their reactions to doing this exercise.

    *Note: Participants usually express feelings of discom-
          fort at being limited to saying "no". The trainer
          will need to help them clarify what else they want
          to communicate to the "asker" besides "no". People
          often want to explain why they are saying "no," or
          want to let the "asker" know they are willing to
          say "yes" at another time. "Requesters" may feel
          hurt or put off by the abruptness and finality of
          a "no" answer.*

6) Saying "no" with phoney excuses; making alternative
    requests. The trainer tells the pairs to continue with
    the same routine, except this time the "refusers" are to
    make up phoney excuses about why they can't do what is
    being asked. Their task is to avoid revealing their
    real reason for saying "no". The "asker" is to be very
    persistent, and to offer alternatives and/or solutions
    to the "refuser's" excuses.

    *Note: The trainer can briefly role play this activity
          with another person.*

    Pairs experiment with this "request and phoney excuse"
    sequence for 2-3 minutes. When the trainer calls time,
    partners switch roles and repeat the exercise.
    (6 minutes)

    *Note: "Refusers" usually find that the "asker's"
          persistence in countering their excuses makes it
          very difficult for them to continue making the
          excuses. Participants discover that the search
          for more and more excuses usually generates an
          anxious "scrambling" plus a feeling of discomfort
          at being dishonest.*

          *Sometimes participants will ask for advice on how
          to deal with the person whose feelings are hurt
          by the refusal, and the group as a whole can
          think of assertive ways to show concern and caring
          for the person without giving up on their decision
          to say "no".*

          *Remind participants that they can choose to
          honestly explain why they are refusing the*

© 1984 Whole Person Press   PO Box 3151   Duluth MN 55803

request, but they don't have to justify their actions.

If there is time, the group may discuss some of the reasons why they are afraid to ask for what they want, or hesitant to say "no" (eg, "They won't like me anymore", or "I'll hurt their feelings", or "I'll be obligated to that person", etc).

8) <u>Assertive requests and refusals.</u> In the third and final part of this exercise, the pairs continue to make and refuse requests, but this time the "refuser" uses one of three assertive responses:
   * "No I won't" or "No I don't want to"
     (no explanation)
   * "No . . . because" (with an honest explanation).
   * "No . . . but" (with possible alternatives).

   When both people have practiced making and refusing requests assertively, they can give each other feedback as to how assertive they were in each role. (10 minutes or more)

9) The trainer asks the entire group to briefly discuss what it was like both to make assertive requests and to experience the clear refusals in Step 8. The group generates a list of situations in which these skills would be particularly effective.

   Participants are encouraged to keep practicing honestly saying "no" (with and without explanation) in their private and/or professional lives whenever they have the opportunity. The trainer notes that once they grow comfortable saying "no", it will probably be easier for them to ask for what they want directly and also to say an unqualified "yes" when they do want to accept.

VARIATION

■ As part of Step 9, participants could use the skills they have practiced in this exercise by role playing with their partners more effective assertive ways of handling their personal list of stressful "requests" and "refusals" which they identified in Step 3.

Submitted by Sandy Christian who adapted this process from an exercise in Lange and Jakubowski, <u>Responsible Assertive Behavior</u> (Champaign IL: Research Press, 1976).

55 AFFIRMATIVE ACTION PLAN

In this attitude-changing exercise participants draw up a plan for using affirmation to manage a workplace stressor.

GOALS

1) To explore the potential of affirmation as a stress management skill.

2) To increase participants' repertoire of affirming behaviors.

3) To develop on-the-job applications for affirmation skills.

GROUP SIZE

Unlimited

TIME FRAME

40-50 minutes

MATERIALS NEEDED

Blackboard or flipchart; "Affirmative Action Plan" worksheets for everyone.

PROCESS

1) The trainer gives some background information on affirmation as a stress reducer, covering some or all of the following points:

- Affirmation is a basic human need. Everyone needs to be touched, recognized and appreciated by other people. Eric Berne popularized this concept by calling it <u>stroke hunger</u>.

- Many work settings are characterized by a highly competitive system where excellence is expected and compliments are few and far between. The need for affirmation or appreciation may be seen as a sign of weakness. Interactions may be calculated to put each other down rather than build each other up. What a pity! There's no substitute for the glow that comes from hearing directly, person-to-person, that you are liked, valued and appreciated by your co-workers.

- Appreciation is often a more influential motivator
  than pay. Most of us will really "put out" just in
  order to hear someone say, "thank you." The
  phenomenal success of "The One Minute Manager" is
  based in part on a simple challenge to managers:
  "Sneak around and catch people doing something good
  -- then tell them about it!"

- Hans Selye, the pioneer stress researcher contends
  that revenge is the most stressful emotion -- and
  gratitude is the healthiest. His personal prescrip-
  tion for managing stress includes cultivating a
  positive attitude and making every day a thanks-
  giving day.

- Cultivating the attitude of gratitude is a double-
  duty stress management strategy. Your positive
  attitude will reduce the stress for the people
  around you -- and probably will reduce your stress
  as well. As an added bonus, appreciation seems to
  be contagious -- once we start giving it freely, it
  often comes back to us full circle.

2) The trainer distributes "Affirmative Action Plan" worksheets to everyone and invites participants to think of
   someone in their work setting who could benefit from
   some additional affirmation (eg, someone you have difficulty relating to; someone you don't particularly
   like; someone who is under a lot of stress or creates a
   lot of stress).

   The trainer directs people to write down the name of
   their chosen co-worker at the top of the worksheet.
   She invites the group to follow along as she leads them
   through a process designed to help them put a little
   sunshine in that person's life.

3) The trainer introduces the first component of the plan,
   acknowledgement, asking the group for ideas about how
   they might simply acknowledge a person's presence or
   existence. All suggestions are listed on the blackboard or newsprint. The trainer elaborates as necessary
   and categorizes the responses into three strategies:

   * Make non-verbal contact (eg, eye contact, smile,
     sitting nearby, etc).
   * Make verbal contact (eg, say "hello," initiate a con-
     versation, tell a joke, ask a question, etc).
   * Pay attention (listen respectfully, ask for input,
     respond to his verbal/non-verbal offerings).

   Participants apply these techniques to their situation

and write down all the potential ways to <u>acknowledge</u>
their chosen person.

*Note: This should be a time for idea-generating, not
making commitments. Encourage participants to
list <u>all</u> actions they <u>could</u> take, not·just those
options they want to or are willing to carry out.
Remind the group to be specific about how, where,
when and how often they could acknowledge this
person.*

4) The trainer invites participants to consider the next
aspect of their plan -- <u>affirmation</u>, which according to
Webster means "responding to in a positive manner" or
"to confirm." The trainer goes on to suggest some basic
affirmation techniques.

* Everyone has some redeeming qualities -- spend
enough time interacting with this person to discover
his strengths.
* Focus on the positive, find something to like about
this person.
* Reinforce what you like, however insignificant --
then disregard everything else.

The trainer challenges the group to think of appropriate
phrases that could communicate affirmation (eg, "I see
what you mean", "That's a good idea", "What an interesting viewpoint", "Tell me more about that!", etc).

Participants are directed to complete the "Affirm" section on their worksheet, answering the questions and
identifying specific ways they could affirm their co-
worker.

5) The trainer invites participants to explore yet another
type of affirmative action -- <u>encouragement</u>, which liter-
ally means "to give courage", but more often is inter-
preted as "giving support." The trainer asks for illus-
trations of how group members like to be supported by
asking,

□ What can other people do for/to you that builds you
up, strengthens you, gives you hope, courage or
support?

Participants give examples of ways they like to be encouraged and the phrases that might accompany such ges-
tures of support (eg, "You did so well last time, this
will be a breeze!", "I know you can do it!", "You're
such a kind soul!", "You've learned a lot about how to
handle this", etc).

The trainer asks participants to turn the tables,
applying what they know about their own need for
encouragement to the person they've chosen to affirm.
They write their responses and potential plans in the
"Encourage" section of the worksheet.

6) The trainer introduces the next dimension of affirmative
action, appreciation, by giving several honest compliments to the group or individual participants (eg, "I've
appreciated your willingness to share", "This is one of
the liveliest groups I've worked with", "I've noticed
that John has helped us stay on track when we wander --
I appreciate your clarity, John.").

The trainer points out some tips for showing appreciation:

- Compliments or praise can show appreciation for
another person's strengths, accomplishments, behavior, appearance, special gifts.

- To be most effective, such positive feedback should
be stated directly to the recipient (eg, "Stuart,
your report was excellent!")

- The best messages of appreciation are also specific,
giving details about the quality, behavior or accom-
plishment you're praising (eg, not only "Your report
was excellent", but also ". . . it was clearly
organized, well-documented and concise. Your choice
of words got the point across without offending any-
one.")

- The impact of a compliment is increased by including
a statement about how the behavior affected you
(eg, "I felt proud of our whole team when you were
done -- your presentation reminded me how well we
cooperated together.")

- Nobody ever really gets tired of hearing honest
compliments, so feel free to show your appreciation
frequently.

Participants again consider their chosen co-worker and
write down several ways they could show their appreciation openly to that person.

7) The trainer directs participants attention to the fifth
method of affirmation, thanks-giving. She notes that all
of us have much to be thankful for and asks participants
to give examples of things in their work setting for
which they are grateful (eg, coffee pot, flexible hours,
secretary who can spell, camaraderie of staff, Christmas
party, electric pencil sharpener, etc).

The trainer notes that even the office ogre makes some contributions that are deserving of thanks. As with appreciation, gratitude is most effective when it is direct, specific and frequent. People love to be thanked over and over again for big favors and small kindnesses. Contrary to popular belief, there's nothing wrong with buttering up the boss -- or the errand boy. In fact, it's likely to be healthy for both of you!

Participants list the various reasons for saying "thank you" to their chosen co-worker.

8) The trainer instructs participants to look over their list of "coulds" and circle (or mark with a star) those affirmative actions they are actually willing to implement. These commitments are revised and rewritten as statements, "I will . . ."

9) Participants are invited to share with the group one or more of their affirmation commitments. The trainer reinforces all suggestions, modeling affirmative action and using these contributions to summarize important points of the session.

   Note: Closing process designs like MANAGER OF THE YEAR (p 98), VITAL SIGNS (Wellness II, p 109) and COPING SKILLS AFFIRMATIONS (Stress I, p 110) give participants an additional opportunity to practice appreciation with each other.

VARIATIONS

■ After Step 8, participants could pair up or rejoin small groups and describe their affirmation plan. Listeners practice their own affirmation skills by giving positive feedback and support.

■ Participants make two affirmative action plans -- one for a co-worker and one for a family member or friend. The group may want to discuss the difference in their affirmation patterns at home versus on the job.

■ Participants could use this same process to make an affirmative action plan for themselves, complete with ideas on how to acknowledge, affirm, encourage, appreciate and thank themselves each day.

■ As part of Step 6, participants could practice giving compliments to others in the group, stating their appreciation for another person's being, doing or sharing and elaborating with details.

AFFIRMATIVE ACTION PLAN

My plan for affirming _____
                                  (Name)

ACKNOWLEDGE: In what ways could you let this person know more
               clearly that you know she/he is living, breathing,
               exists, etc. What little things could you do to
               pay attention to this person?

               I could . . .

AFFIRM: How and when could you respond in a positive manner
               to this person? What thoughts, opinions, beliefs,
               does she/he hold that you could confirm as true?
               What positive phrases could you use more often?

               I could . . .

ENCOURAGE: In what ways could you give this person suport even
               if you're in disagreement? What might enhance this
               person's self-confidence? What does she/he need
               to hear to feel strengthened to tackle the day?

               I could . . .

APPRECIATE: What are some of this person's strengths that you
                  value? When could you honestly praise him/her?
                  What compliments could you give?

                  I could . . .

GIVE THANKS: What contributions does this person make for which
                  you are grateful? When could you say "thank you?"

                  I could . . .

I WILL:

56 ANCHORING

Participants guide one another through a relaxation fantasy and "anchor" the comfortable feelings they experience for later recall and stimulation of the relaxation response.

GOALS

1) To develop a quick self-eliciting resource for relaxation.

2) To demonstrate the potency of recalled experience in creating responses.

GROUP SIZE

Unlimited

TIME FRAME

30 minutes

MATERIALS NEEDED

A copy of "Instructions for Guides" and "Instructions for Followers" for each participant.

PROCESS

1) The trainer describes the relationship between stress and relaxation using the S-R model outlined below:

   The stress response is elicited by whatever cues we perceive as threatening (eg, a near-accident, a noise in the dark house, a final exam). Even past experiences we recall or fantasy experiences that never occurred can elicit the stress response.

   The relaxation response is also stimulated by certain cues (eg, music, watching the ocean, lying in the sun, a soothing touch, etc). The relaxation response can also be elicited by past experiences we recall and by fantasy experiences that we imagine.

   Each individual is free to choose which cues to attend to. We can choose to respond to cues that elicit relaxation rather than cues that promote stress. We can also purposefully train ourselves to relax in response to a specific cue.

2)   The trainer explains the purpose of the exercise -- to
     connect a series of relaxing experiences/images to a
     spot on the body. This process is called "anchoring".
     Subsequently touching this spot acts as a cue for elici-
     ting the relaxation response.

3)   Participants pair up and distribute themselves around
     the room. Partners will be training one another in the
     anchoring technique.

4)   The trainer distributes the "Instructions for Guides"
     and "Instructions for Followers" to all participants.
     One partner is the "guide" first. The other partner is
     the "follower". The trainer briefly describes the pro-
     cess, then allows the pairs to read their instructions
     thoroughly. The trainer answers any questions and then
     directs participants to proceed at their own pace.

     *Note: The trainer should wander around the room quietly
            offering assistance or clarification as needed.*

5)   After 10 minutes, the trainer signals the "guides" that
     time is up. The partners debrief and check the anchor-
     ing response as indicated on their instructions. Then
     they change roles and repeat the process. (10-15 minutes)

     *Note: Be sure to allow time for the "followers" to de-
            scribe their experience to their partners before
            switching roles and moving on.*

6)   When all participants have completed the practice, the
     trainer may reconvene the group and ask people to share
     their experiences. (5 minutes)

7)   Participants are encouraged to "pile up" even more
     experiences on the anchor by touching it whenever they
     feel particularly relaxed (eg, hot bath, sunset, sitting
     by the fire).

VARIATION

■ A related technique called "spot checking" uses a visual
  cue to elicit relaxation. The process for "spot checking"
  remains as outlined above for "anchoring" except participants in this case anchor the relaxation experience visually
  to a small colored adhesive dot (available at office supply
  stores). The dots are then placed by the person at strate-
  gic locations (phone, typewriter, watch, wallet) as a visual
  reminder to relax.

Submitted by David X. Swenson

© 1984 Whole Person Press   PO Box 3151   Duluth MN 55803

INSTRUCTIONS FOR GUIDES

1) Begin by asking your partner to show you the exact spot she wants you to use as an "anchor" for her relaxed feelings.

2) Ask your partner to find a comfortable, balanced posture (seated, lying, leaning against the wall). Once she is settled ask her to take a deep breath, close her eyes and relax. Tell her to focus on breathing and let go of any tension she feels. Instruct her to continue breathing deeply and to nod her head when she feels quite relaxed.

3) As soon as she nods her head, you are going to help her recall an especially relaxing experience. Your job is to help her make it vivid in her imagination. Your instructions need to guide her in the process, yet be general enough so that she can create the scene for herself.

   You will need to go slowly, allowing time for the images to form in her mind. A nod is always a signal that she is ready to move on.

4) Start by saying, "I'd like you to recall a deeply relaxing situation from your personal experience, a time when you felt extremely calm and at peace. Remember everything you can about that time of peaceful relaxation. Bring it alive in your mind."

   While your partner is imaging, you can heighten the sensory visualization by suggesting she notice the colors, hues, shapes and contrasts in her image. After a pause you might suggest that she pay attention to the sounds and smells, the temperature, the feeling of the scene around her.

   All these suggestions should be made in very general terms so your partner can create the specifics of her scenario without your preferences sneaking in. Try permissive language such as "you might notice". Use words suggesting relaxation such as "comfortable", "restful", "easy", "calm", "peaceful".

5) When the experience is quite realistic and eliciting peak relaxation, your partner should nod. At this point, you should touch the anchor spot on her hand.

6) Ask your partner to recall another relaxing experience or ask her to create in fantasy the most relaxing scene she could possibly imagine. Repeat Steps 4 and 5, helping her enrich the scene with sensory images and anchoring the response to her "spot" when the experience is most intense.

7) Repeat Step 4 and Step 5 with a third relaxation fantasy.

8) Ask your partner to return her awareness outside herself again, back to your interaction. Give her a minute or two to get reoriented and then ask her to describe her experience to you.

9) Sometime during her description reach over and touch the anchor spot to test if it really elicits relaxation.

INSTRUCTIONS FOR FOLLOWERS

Your guide is going to help you visualize a series of especially relaxing scenes from your personal experience or fantasy.

During this experience you will need a silent signal to communicate with your partner. Just nod your head to let him know when you have an image clearly in mind and are experiencing peak relaxation.

You also need to choose a spot on your body for your partner to use as an "anchor" point for these relaxation visualizations. Most people choose a spot near the knuckle of the index finger. Your guide will touch this spot for you when you indicate peak relaxation. Later you can touch this same spot to elicit feelings of relaxation for yourself.

You will be visualizing two or three scenes. Each time you feel yourself relaxing totally into the mood of the scene you will nod to your guide and he will touch you on the anchor spot. This will add each subsequent relaxation experience to those already "anchored" to that spot. When your time is up, describe your experience as completely as you can, paying special attention to the signs of relaxation you notice.

Before you switch roles and become the guide, touch your anchor spot yourself and notice the response.

Remember, you can add more of your own calming experiences to this special spot by touching your anchor point whenever you're feeling particularly relaxed. Then, when you're under stress, just take a deep breath, touch the anchor point and the relaxing images will again flood into your being.

57 THE ABC'S OF TIME

This skill-building exercise illustrates the importance of spending time where it counts. Participants list the activities and tasks that consumed yesterday's 24 hours, then assess whether or not they invested effort in their top priorities.

GOALS

1) To help participants identify how they spend their time.

2) To distinguish the "A" priorities from the "B" and "C" tasks.

3) To understand and practice the major time-use skills.

GROUP SIZE

Unlimited

TIME FRAME

40-50 minutes

MATERIALS NEEDED

A copy of "Yesterday's Time Log Analysis" for each participant; "Each Day is a New Account" script.

PROCESS

A) Time-Use Analysis

1) The trainer distributes "Yesterday's Time Log Analysis" worksheets and instructs participants to complete Columns I and II. (10 minutes)

   Note: Participants should recall the details of yesterday's schedule as completely as possible -- what they did, when, who they talked with, about what, etc.

   They are to estimate as accurately as possible the time spent on each activity. Participants are to account for all 24 hours of the day. If they end up with large blocks of time not accounted for, it may be a sign that they wasted a good share of the day simply spinning their wheels.

2)   The trainer outlines the following A, B, C time-use
     ranking system. As he describes each category, the
     trainer asks the group for examples of activities from
     their lists that fit that priority.

       ● "A's" are those tasks and activities that are re-
         lated to your major priorities and are connected to
         your life goals.

       ● "B's" are the tasks that must be done, but do not
         seem to be life-goal related. Every day we com-
         plete tasks which must be done in order to give us
         the opportunity to move toward life goals (eg, mak-
         ing a living - "B", in order to provide for your
         family - "A".)

       ● "C's" are the activities that add very little if
         anything to one's life. Like third class mail,
         these time-wasters clutter up our existence and
         quickly eat up our days.

     Participants rate each of their categories according to
     these priorities (Column III)

3)   In Column IV participants list all of yesterday's "A"
     activities and total the number of hours spent on "A's".
     They divide this number by 24 to compute the percentage
     of time spent on "As" (Column IV).

4)   Participants then respond to the first three questions
     on the lower half of the worksheet, writing their
     answers on the back or on a blank sheet of paper.

B)   The Skill of Using the ABC's

5)   The trainer shares guidelines for using the ABC's of
     time management, including some or all of the following
     points:

       ● Every day, no matter how "busy" or tired, make sure
         you spend at least five minutes working directly on
         a life goal. Build in time for your "A's" -- EVERY
         DAY! Plan it into the schedule. If nothing happens
         in a day, nothing happens!

       ● Complete only as many "B's" as you must in order to
         give yourself the opportunity to keep working on
         your "A's".

- Everytime a "C" comes into your life, throw it in a cardboard box. At the end of the month, throw the box in the garbage without even peeking. Ignore the "C's". If you mislabel a "C", it will come back at you as a "B". (eg, if you label your Mastercard bill a "C" priority one month, a call from the credit department will probably move it up to a "B" next month!)

- It's tempting to "click off" the "C's" rather than tackle the "A's" since "C's" are easy and quick to complete. Although this helps you feel like you've accomplished something, all you've really done is to stay busy! Spend time moving toward goals instead of just filling hours or crossing unimportant items off your list.

- Don't always work at other people's "A's" instead of your own.

- When you keep your priorities clearly in mind throughout the day, you manage your stress instead of letting it manage you.

- To make your time count, your life count, yourself count -- spend yourself, your life and your time where it counts!

6) The trainer may read the "Each Day is a New Account" essay, as a challenge to the group.

7) Participants respond to the last two questions at the bottom of the worksheet.

VARIATIONS

- As part of Step 7 participants form groups of three and compare insights about their time use patterns and resolutions for change. This is an ideal way for people to discover that everyone's priorities are different!

TRAINER'S NOTES

YESTERDAY'S TIME LOG ANALYSIS

■ Mentally think through the events of yesterday. List all the
  ways you spent your time <u>yesterday</u> (24 hours). Be as specific
  and as accurate as possible. Use 1/4 hour segments. Be sure
  to total 24 hours! Keep thinking until you account for the
  whole day. Recall the specific details of yesterday's schedule, being as precise as possible (eg, ate breakfast; picked
  up kitchen; dictation; watched television; talked with the
  kids, staff, spouse; went to the dentist; read the paper, mail,
  book; listened to music; exercised; wrote proposal; thought
  about . . .; etc).

I Tasks/ Activities	II Time Spent (Hours)	III Priority Ranking A B C

IV
List All "A" Items
Item   Time   Spent

Total Time Spent on
"A" Activities

☐ hours

Percentage of Time
Spent on "A"
(Divide total by 24)

☐ %

■ Was yesterday typical? In what ways "yes"? In what ways "no"?
■ What do you applaud about your use of time yesterday? What do
  you deplore?
■ What would you like to do differently?

■ How could you put more "A" time into your day?
■ How will you start making that happen now?

EACH DAY IS A NEW ACCOUNT

If you had a bank that credited your account each morning
with $86,000 . . .

That carried over no balance from day to day . . .

Allowed you to keep no cash in your accounts . . .

And every evening cancelled whatever part of the amount
you had failed to use during the day . . .

What would you do?

Draw out every cent every day, of course, and use it
to your advantage!

Well, you have such a bank . . . and its name is "TIME."

Every morning, it credits you with 86,400 seconds.
Every night, it writes off as lost whatever of this you
have failed to invest to good purpose.

It carries over no balances.

It allows no overdrafts.

Each day, it opens a new account with you.

Each night, it burns the records of the day.

If you fail to use the day's deposits, the loss is
yours.

There is no going back.

There is no drawing against the "Tomorrow."

It is up to each of us to invest this precious fund
of hours, minutes and seconds in order to get from it
the utmost in health, happiness and success!

From The Stress Examiner © Aid Association for Lutherans, 1982.

ACTION PLANNING/CLOSURE

58 PERSONAL/PROFESSIONAL REVIEW (p 97)

Participants review the session and affirm what they have gained
from the learning experience.   (10-15 minutes)

59 MANAGER OF THE YEAR (p 98)

In this closing affirmation participants write recommendations for
themselves and campaign for "Stress Manager of the Year"
awards.   (45-60 minutes)

60 GOALS, OBSTACLES AND ACTIONS (p 102)

This in-depth planning exercise helps participants set goals,
formulate strategies for moving toward their goals, and monitor
their progress.   (60 minutes)

61 25 WORDS OR LESS (p 108)

Participants exchange advice for managing stress.
(10-15 minutes)

62 STRESS AND COPING JOURNAL (p 110)

This on-going homework assignment helps participants monitor
their stress and apply the management techniques learned
during a several week course.
(5-10 minutes; three 15-30 minute homework periods)

58 PERSONAL/PROFESSIONAL REVIEW

Participants review the session and affirm what they have gained from the learning experience.

GOALS

1) To promote application of concepts and transfer of learning to real life situations.

2) To end the session on a positive note.

GROUP SIZE

Unlimited; if the group is larger than 20, divide into small groups of 6-12 persons.

TIME FRAME

10-15 minutes

PROCESS

Note: This exercise is most effective at the end of a session or workshop where PERSONAL/PROFESSIONAL (p 2) is used as an icebreaker.

1) The trainer invites participants to reflect on the topics and activities of the day or session. She asks them to make a mental list of what they have learned about stress and coping, and about themselves.

2) Participants take turns sharing their responses to the following sentence stems:

   * One thing I gained <u>personally</u> from this session. . .
   * One thing I gained <u>professionally</u> (or for my work setting) . . .

   Note: With more than 20 participants, divide into smaller groups (6-12 persons) for Step 2.

3) The trainer summarizes the variety of learnings expressed and highlights any important issues that were not mentioned.

VARIATION

■ The trainer may want to enhance the transfer value by asking participants to state one specific application for each learning they identify.

---

59 MANAGER OF THE YEAR

In this closing affirmation participants write recommendations for themselves and campaign for "Stress Manager of
the Year" awards.

GOALS

1) To enhance self-perceptions of competence for dealing
with stress.

2) To provide closure for the learning experience.

3) To promote positive feedback among participants.

GROUP SIZE

Works best with 12-25 people.

TIME FRAME

45-60 minutes, depending on group size and creativity.

MATERIALS NEEDED

Blank paper or "Nomination Memo" worksheets for everyone.
"Campaign Guidelines" for each small group. A "Campaign Kit"
for each group -- a large bag filled with arts and crafts
supplies such as newsprint, balloons, posterboard, crepe
paper, blank buttons or name tags, string, straws, note-
cards, paper cups and plates, tape, glue, scissors, magic
markers, etc. "Stress Manager of the Year" certificates
for all.

PROCESS

*Note: This exercise is more fun if there is plenty of time
for the creative campaign activities suggested. Although more "sophisticated" groups may initially resist
such "childish" projects, most people eventually get
caught up in the flow and find the process quite energizing and enlightening.*

1) The trainer distributes "Nomination Memo" worksheets
and announces that every participant is a candidate for
the "Stress Manager of the Year Award." Each person is
to write a memo of recommendation for himself, describing tough situations he has managed well, coping techniques he uses often and/or skillfully, new strategies he
has learned and practiced during this course.

> *Note: Some people may balk at such blatant self-*
> *aggrandizement. Reassure them that bragging this*
> *one time won't ruin their credibility or com-*
> *promise their humility. Public affirmation of*
> *successful coping experiences is a powerful rein-*
> *forcer and motivator for positive stress management*
> *in the future.*

2) If small sharing groups have been utilized during the
   learning experience, the trainer instructs participants
   to rejoin the most recent group. If not, participants
   are directed to form three person groups for this segment of the exercise.

   Each person in turn reads his memo of recommendation to
   the others in his group. They are then free to add their
   positive comments to the recommendation, noting how they
   have observed him coping well with stress -- inside or
   outside of class. This feedback is recorded on the memo
   in the form of a P.S. and signed by the person who made
   the comment. (10-15 minutes)

3) When all group members have completed their turns, a
   representative is sent to the trainer who gives her a
   copy of the "Campaign Guidelines" and a "Campaign Kit."
   The group plans a campaign for themselves as "Stress
   Managers of the Year" following the guidelines and uses
   the art materials to prepare a "floor demonstration" for
   the rally. (30 minutes)

4) The trainer reconvenes the group and sets the stage for
   a campaign rally. Each "delegation" is invited to take
   the floor for a brief "demonstration," parading their
   campaign creations, singing their song, shouting their
   slogans. The audience is encouraged to respond with enthusiastic applause, cheers and flag waving.

5) The trainer distributes a certificate suitable for
   framing to each participant designating her as "Stress
   Manager of the Year."

VARIATION

■ If group members know each other well, they could draw names
  or choose partners and write memos of recommendation for
  each other instead of for themselves.

NOMINATION MEMO

TO: Selection Committee

RE: Stress Manager of the Year Award Nomination:

_____
(name)

MY LETTER OF RECOMMENDATION

CAMPAIGN GUIDELINES

You have 30 minutes to devise a campaign for this group as
"Stress Managers of the Year." Make sure that everyone is included in all parts of the campaign planning and preparation.

Start by listing your common stressors and the coping strengths
the people in your group have demonstrated.

Decide on a name for yourselves that reflects your stress or
affirms your management style (eg, "The Vegetarians", "The
Parents of Adolescents", "The Type AB's", "The Support Staff
Supporters", etc).

Brainstorm together a number of slogans that describe your suc-
cessful stress management styles or specific strategies you
recommend for others (eg, "A mile a day keeps the blues away!"
or "Eat, drink and be merry - in moderation only." or "Ban the
butts." or "Work groups who play together stay together.").

Make up a theme song for yourselves, if you have time.

Use the supplies in your "Campaign Kit" to make posters, balloons,
placards, symbols, banners, awards, mementos, hats, badges, etc
for use in promoting your group at the managers of the year rally.
Have fun! Be wild, zany and creative! Most of all, be affirming
of each other and your accomplishments.

© 1984 Whole Person Press PO Box 3151 Duluth MN 55803

60 GOALS, OBSTACLES AND ACTIONS

This in-depth planning exercise helps participants set goals, formulate strategies for moving toward their goals, and monitor their progress.

GOALS

1) To help participants identify a limited number of specific behavior change goals.

2) To formulate a plan of action for overcoming the obstacles that hold them back, and to monitor their step-by-step progress toward their goals.

GROUP SIZE

Unlimited; also effective in work with individuals.

TIME FRAME

60 minutes

MATERIALS NEEDED

Blank paper and two or three "Goals, Obstacles, Actions" worksheets for each person.

PROCESS

A) Formulating The Goals

1) On a blank sheet of paper, participants write down a list of personal goals related to the course/workshop. Participants may record as many ideas as they like.

   Note: Use whatever warm-up seems appropriate, based on the style and content of the course. You may want to review the subjects covered, and ask participants to peruse their own notes. Or, if participants have kept a running "wish list" (Wellness II, p 52), have them refer to this list as they begin selecting their goals.

2) The trainer asks participants to reflect on their initial list of goals based on the following criteria.

   Note: Be sure to give participants enough time between questions to register their responses.

□ Are these your own goals, or are they expectations
someone else has set for you? Cross out those that
are not fully your own.

□ Are the goals realistic and attainable? Cross out
those that you believe are impossible for you now.

□ Are they stated positively? (eg, "I want to quit
smoking" is stated negatively. The positive goal
is "I want to be a non-smoker!") Rephrase your
goals into positive statements of intention.

□ Are you willing to begin working right now to
achieve these goals? Cross out all those to which
you respond "no." Hold them for some later date.

3) The trainer asks participants to select 1-3 goals for
further in-depth work, and to list those goals selected
on a second sheet of paper.

*Note: For this exercise the maximum number of goals
should be three -- one or two would be preferable.*

4) The trainer asks participants to refine their goals by
responding to the following issues:

*Note: Give participants enough time between questions
to register their responses.*

□ Make each general goal very specific -- what, when,
where. (eg, "I want to be happier" is a goal, but
it's not specific. "To be happier, I want to
improve my relationship with Bob" is specific.)

□ Check whether the specific wants are consistent
with your belief system -- your values, self-concept,
long-range goals, commitments, etc. If not, modify
the goal or cross it off your list.

□ For each specific goal answer the following ques-
tions:
   * What might I have to give up in order to reach
     this goal?
   * Am I willing to give this up?
   * What parts of this goal don't I want to touch
     right now?
   * What moves might I be willing to make now?

B) Confronting The Barriers

  5) The trainer instructs participants to write one of
      their specific goals in the upper left hand corner of a
      "Goals, Obstacles, Actions" worksheet. Participants
      use a separate worksheet for each of their goals.

  6) For each goal, participants list all the roadblocks and
      obstacles that have kept them from reaching this goal
      in the past. They respond to the questions in Column 1,
      "Obstacles and Roadblocks," writing as many responses as
      occur to them.
         □ Why have I not already achieved this?
         □ What's stopping me?

  7) Participants then list possible solutions for overcoming
      each separate obstacle and record these ideas in
      Column 2, "Possible Solutions."

      *Note: Participants complete Steps 2 and 3 of Part B
             for each separate goal before moving on to Part C.*

C) Formulating The Action Plan

  8) In Column 2, participants circle all activities they will
      perform in order to remove each barrier and move toward
      their goal(s).

  9) Participants determine the specific timing for each
      activity to which they are committing themselves. (What
      will they do? When? Where? How often? For how long?)
      They record this information in Column 3, "Timing."

  10) The trainer challenges participants to identify a re-
      ward they will experience or give themselves when they
      have successfully completed each activity. These are
      recorded in Column 4, "Rewards."

  11) To clarify their action plan, participants complete the
      sentence stems at the bottom of the worksheet.

      *Note: Participants complete Steps 1-4 of Part C for
             each goal.*

D) <u>Monitoring The Progress</u>

12) Participants set specific appointments (daily, weekly, monthly) with themselves for monitoring their perform- ance and for evaluating the success of each activity. They mark these dates on their calendar.

Note: Remind participants to reward themselves for following through on their plans, even if the goal is not reached. After all, the plan was only an "estimate" of what might help them achieve the goal. However, participants are not to reward themselves for planned activities they never complete -- even if the goal was reached!

13) When evaluating their progress at the appointed time(s), participants are encouraged to mark down dates when activities were accomplished, revise plans as necessary for unfinished goals, set new goals and begin again. They record their progress in <u>Column 5</u> of the worksheet or in a separate journal.

Note: After the initial weekly or monthly checkpoints are completed, participants are to continue to replan at least once each year, and to reward themselves for whatever positive change they have maintained. They may want to select a special day such as their birthday, anniversary or New Year's Eve for this yearly checkup.

It is important for future reference that partici- pants track all progress in writing, and record the results of these "performance checks" in a log book of their choosing.

Inform participants that if they temporarily go off course, they are not failures! Encourage people to re-examine their goals. If they no longer desire the goal, drop it! If they are still intent on reaching it, they should analyze what went haywire, learn from the difficulty they've faced and formulate a new plan of action -- in writing!

TRAINER'S NOTES

© 1984 Whole Person Press   PO Box 3151 Duluth MN 55803

GOALS, OBSTACLES,

GOAL _____

1) OBSTACLES AND ROADBLOCKS	2) POSSIBLE SOLUTIONS AND ACTIVITIES PLAN OUTLINE
Why have I not already achieved this? What's stopping me?	How could I overcome these obstacles by using my strengths and resources?
	A
	B
	C
	A
	B
	C
	A
	B
	C
	A
	B
	C
	A
	B
	C

As I reach toward this goal I will be/have more:

ACTIONS

3) TIMING	4) REWARDS I WILL EXPERIENCE	5) TRACKING PROGRESS
By when, how many times, time of day etc.	Intrinsic benefits, self rewards	Completed by:

Detailed comments and notes on my plan to reach this goal:

61 25 WORDS OR LESS

Participants exchange advice for managing stress.

GOALS

1) To help participants articulate what they have learned about stress management.

2) To add drama, suspense and energy to the transfer-of-learning process.

GROUP SIZE

Works best with 8-40 people.

TIME FRAME

10-15 minutes; more with larger groups

MATERIALS NEEDED

3" x 5" index cards for all participants.
For variations: Blank stamped postcards, magic markers, crayons, colored pencils, stickers, etc.

PROCESS

1) The trainer announces that participants have finally attained the status of stress management experts and will now have a chance to demonstrate their wisdom. He distributes a 3" x 5" notecard to everyone with the following instructions:

> Please write down in 25 words or less, your response to the question, "What is your best advice for managing stress?"

2) The trainer collects all the cards and mixes them up. One-by-one each participant is invited to choose a card and read out loud the "words to the wise" written on it.

3) Participants are encouraged to take their chosen advice card home, display it in a prominent place, read it at least once a day and heed whatever advice it gives.

VARIATIONS

■ Paragraphs of advice could be written on a postcard and decorated with drawings, doodles, designs or stickers.

Each participant writes her name and address on her card.
The trainer collects the cards and sends them to participants at a later date (one week, one month, six months) for
posting on the refrigerator, mirror or bulletin board as a
reminder.

■ The trainer (or someone in the group) could collect all
advice cards, type up everyone's suggestions, duplicate the
list and distribute it to all as a "Primer on Stress Management."

TRAINER'S NOTES

62 STRESS AND COPING JOURNAL

This on-going homework assignment helps participants monitor their stress and apply the management techniques learned during a several week course.

GOALS

1) To facilitate application of concepts to real-life situations.

2) To monitor stress levels and progress in implementation of coping skills.

GROUP SIZE

Any size; a good tool for use with individuals as well.

TIME FRAME

5-10 minutes; three 15-30 minute homework periods.

MATERIALS NEEDED

Copies of the "Stress and Coping Journal Format" for everyone; participants will also need to obtain their own journals or notebooks.

PROCESS

1) The trainer introduces the concept of a stress diary or journal as a useful tool for documenting stress-provoking situations, monitoring reactions and tracking the effectiveness of management strategies.

2) The trainer distributes "Stress and Coping Journal Formats," commenting that each journal entry should be written narrative style and include responses to all three areas indicated on the format. Participants are directed to obtain a notebook and keep a journal for the next week (or whatever period between sessions). They are to write in the journal at least three times a week.

   Note: The trainer may read an excerpt from her own journal as an example, but will also want to underscore the reality that each person's style can and should be unique.

3) The trainer collects the journals a day or two before the next class. She reviews the contents and then

returns them to participants at the class.   The journal is then used again for recording observations during the next week.

Note: For maximum benefit to participants, the trainer should read each journal thoroughly and write comments that give feedback on stress and coping skills. Be generous with affirmation as people experiment with new behaviors.

TRAINER'S NOTES

Submitted by Mary O'Brien Sippel

STRESS AND COPING JOURNAL FORMAT

This journal is a tool to help you record significant information about the stress in your life, your coping style and how you
apply to your life situations what you've learned in class.

Be sure to write in your journal at least three times during the
week. Record objective specifics (dates, times, activities, etc)
as well as your observations, thoughts, feelings etc. Write each
entry on the same day that the experience you are describing
occurred.

- Describe the day's experiences with special attention to
  any aspect of the day that was particularly stressful or
  exciting.

- Relate the topics discussed in the last class to the
  stress of this day.

- Recount the various coping skills you used during the day
  to manage this stress or to view it differently. Comment
  on the effectiveness of each strategy.

GROUP ENERGIZERS

63 THE GARDEN

This poignant parable focuses on the difference between "play" and "scoring."

GOALS

1) To help participants reflect on the purpose of life, interactions with others and play.

TIME FRAME

5 minutes

PROCESS

1) The trainer reads the parable, "The Garden."

THE GARDEN

In the beginning, God didn't make just two people, he made a bunch of us. Because he wanted us to have a lot of fun, and he said you can't really have fun unless there's a whole gang of you. He put us in Eden which was a combination garden and playground and park and told us to have fun.

At first we did have fun just like he expected. We rolled down the hills, waded in the streams, climbed on the trees, swung on the vines, ran in the meadows, frolicked in the woods, hid in the forest, and acted silly. We laughed a lot.

Then one day this snake told us that we weren't having real fun because we weren't keeping score. Back then, we didn't know what score was. When he explained it, we still couldn't see the fun. But he said we should give an apple to the person who was best at all the games and we'd never know who was best without keeping score. We could all see the fun of that, of course, because we were all sure we were best.

It was different after that. We yelled a lot. We had to make up new scoring rules for most of the games. Others, like frolicking, we stopped playing because they were too hard to score.

By the time God found out what had happened we were spending about 45 minutes a day actually playing and the rest of the time working out scoring. God was

wroth about that -- very, very wroth. He said we
couldn't use his garden anymore because we weren't
having fun. We told him we were having lots of fun.
He was just being narrowminded because it wasn't ex-
actly the kind of fun he originally thought of.

He wouldn't listen.

He kicked us out, and he said we couldn't come back until we stopped keeping score. To rub it in (to get our
attention, he said), he told us we were all going to
die and our scores wouldn't mean anything anyway.

He was wrong. My cumulative, all-game score now is
16,548 and that means a lot to me. If I can raise it
to 20,000 before I die, I'll know I've accomplished
something. Even if I can't, my life has a great deal
of meaning because I've taught my children to score
high and they'll be able to reach 20,000 or even 30,000.

Really, it was life in the garden that didn't mean anything. Fun is great in its place but without scoring
there's no reason for it. God actually has a very
superficial view of life and I'm certainly glad my
children are being raised away from his influence. We
were lucky. We're all very grateful to the snake.

2)   The trainer asks participants to identify a specific
     instance when they turned "play" into the "scoring
     achievement syndrome" and a specific instance when they
     played "simply for the fun of it."

3)   The trainer encourages participants to search out and
     treasure those moments when they are able to let down
     their guard, let go of responsibility and turn off the
     scoreboard in their heads. (Family reunion, holding an
     infant, laughing with others, watching a parade, etc)

VARIATION

■ This reading serves as a wonderful warm-up for THE MONTH OF
  FUNDAYS (p 61).

The author of this story is Ann Herbert -- so our dog-eared copy
says. Someone gave it to us years ago with no reference but Ann's
name. In workshops across the country we've asked, "Who and where
is Ann Herbert?" but so far no one has known. It's a beautiful
parable that has touched many. Will the real Ann Herbert please
stand up!

64 HAND-TO-HAND CONTACT

In this soothing relaxation break participants trade hand massages. This technique is especially effective for people who use their fingers and hands for extended periods or those who experience chronic discomfort in these areas.

GOALS

1) To reduce tension in fingers and hands.

2) To provide a non-threatening experience that facilitates the learning of a massage procedure.

GROUP SIZE

Unlimited

TIME FRAME

10 minutes

MATERIALS NEEDED

"Hand Massage" handout

PROCESS

1) The trainer introduces this energizer by describing briefly the effect of finger and hand tension on the total body. The trainer points out that massage is an ideal technique for reducing some of that tension -- by helping muscles relax and stimulating increased blood supply to the area.

2) The trainer asks participants to pair up with a neighbor for a refreshing relaxation break. She distributes "Hand Massage" handouts and participants follow along as she describes the process of hand massage.

   Note: The trainer may want to demonstrate the process with a volunteer. Be sure to show the different kinds of strokes that are used (eg, thumb circles, subtle back and forth motions with fingertips, long sweeps, gentle pulling on fingers, kneading, etc). Encourage participants to practice on their own hands, experimenting with a variety of strokes and pressures.

© 1984   Whole Person Press   PO Box 3151   Duluth MN 55803

3) Partners decide who will be the first receiver. The trainer talks the whole group slowly through the massage, using the instructions on the handout. The process is repeated on the other hand, with the trainer directing the pace.

> *Note: Overhead projection of the hand massage diagram provides a hands-free ready reference for the masseur.*

4) Partners switch roles and repeat Step 3.

5) The trainer may ask for comments and observations. She reminds participants that self-massage is a relaxation technique they can use whenever and wherever they need tension relief -- finding a friend to exchange with doubles the benefits!

VARIATION

- This exercise can be taught as a "do-it-yourself" process, rather than a shared experience.

TRAINER'S NOTES

Genie L Wessel submitted this routine which is based on a hand massage technique she learned from John Davis at the University of Maryland.

HAND MASSAGE

RECEIVER:

1) Begin by warming and increasing the electric field between
    your hands. Slowly rub your palms together for 1-2 minutes.

GIVER:

2) Take one of the receiver's hands between your two hands; hold
    it gently.
3) Circle the wrist with both your hands; hold for 60 seconds.
4) Proceed by:

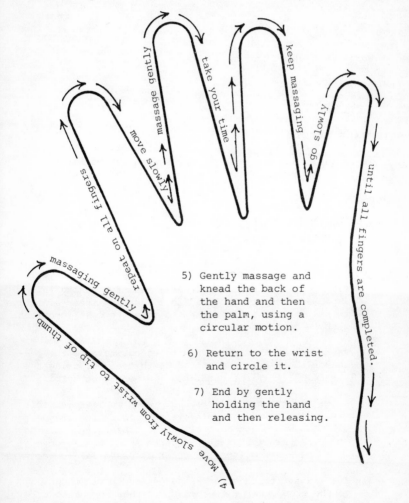

5) Gently massage and
   knead the back of
   the hand and then
   the palm, using a
   circular motion.

6) Return to the wrist
   and circle it.

7) End by gently
   holding the hand
   and then releasing.

65 HELPERS ANONYMOUS

In this tongue-in-cheek initiation rite, participants con-
fess their addiction to helping and learn the HA theme song.

GOALS

1) To encourage participants to laugh at a stress-producing
   habit.

2) To remind participants that their wants and needs are
   important.

GROUP SIZE

Works best with 20 or more people.

TIME FRAME

5 minutes

MATERIALS NEEDED

Newsprint, transparency or handout with lyrics for the
"Helpers Anonymous Theme Song".

PROCESS

*Note: This exercise is a perfect companion to HOOKED ON
     HELPING (p 39).*

1) The trainer introduces the exercise by welcoming all
   the new members of Helper's Anonymous to this initiation meeting. He congratulates them for taking this
   important step on the road to conquering their addiction
   to helping and invites them to take the next important
   step -- confession.

2) Participants are instructed to stand, turn to the person on their left and introduce themselves, using the
   phrase, "I'm (first name) and I'm hooked on helping."

   *Note: The trainer will probably want to liven up this
        step to help people overcome their resistance.
        Suggest hand on heart while confessing. Remind
        the group that the Helper's Anonymous acronym --
        HA -- encourages laughter as essential to recovery.*

3) The trainer teaches the Helper's Anonymous Theme Song
   to the group, using newsprint, overhead or handouts

for the lyrics. The group sings the song once in unison
complete with the actions indicated.

*Note: The trainer will need to help people get into the
        swing of things by dramatically modeling the
        pointing actions and encouraging the group to
        exaggerate their motions.*

4) After everyone has learned the theme song, the trainer
   divides the group into four sections for singing in
   rounds. The sections sing the song through three times,
   singing the 3 first lines more softly each time and the
   last 3 lines more loudly. The last time through, the
   groups whisper the first lines and shout the last one!

HELPER'S ANONYMOUS THEME SONG

(Tune: "Frère Jacques")

Hooked on helping, hooked on helping!
Care for you! (point to someone)
And you, too! (point to someone else)

No more one-way giving, (wag finger)
Time for healthy living! (point to watch)
I count, too! I count, too! (point to self)

Original lyrics by Nancy Loving Tubesing

© 1984 Whole Person Press   PO Box 3151   Duluth MN 55803

66 MUSICAL MOVEMENT

A montage of musical styles provides the background and beat for tension-reducing interpretive movement.

GOALS

1) To expand awareness of the value of music and movement as coping techniques.

2) To provide a playful interlude.

GROUP SIZE

Unlimited, as long as the space is adequate.

TIME FRAME

10-15 minutes; can easily be expanded.

MATERIALS NEEDED

Record or cassette player with various instrumental recordings.

PROCESS

1) The trainer introduces this exercise with a few comments on the power of music to evoke a variety of moods and feelings. The combination of music and body movement can be energizing or relaxing or both.

2) Participants are invited to stand and spread themselves around the room so everyone has space to move freely. The trainer asks everyone to close their eyes, take a few deep breaths, let their minds clear and tune in to their bodies.

3) After a moment or two of silent concentration, the trainer turns on the music and suggests that participants listen closely, allowing the music to flow into their bodies.

    Note: *Start with an irresistible tune and beat such as a Sousa march, William Tell Overture, Kay Gardner, Tiajuana Brass, Star Wars, Chariots of Fire, Strauss Waltz, or a current rock hit.*

4) The trainer encourages participants to start moving with the music. Keeping their eyes closed, everyone

begins interpreting the music -- swaying, rocking,
dancing, stretching, spinning, marching -- whatever
the beat prompts them to do.

> *Note: Some people may need extra encouragement to loosen
> up and enjoy this exercise. The trainer could
> suggest specific movements to try (clap, snap
> fingers, tap feet, skip, twist and turn, wave
> arms, etc). Remind the group to hear the beat
> and let their bodies keep time.*

5) Steps 3 and 4 are repeated several times, each time
using a different musical selection (slow, fast, loud,
soft, jazz, classical, folk, etc).

VARIATIONS

- One person can lead the group in follow-the-leader interpretive movements.

- Participants pair up and interpret the first musical selection together. For the second selection, two dyads join
together and move to the music as quartets. Two quartets
join and work together as a group of eight to interpret the
next selection. This doubling process is continued until
the entire group is involved in a giant communal dance.

TRAINER'S NOTES

67 ROUND OF APPLAUSE

In this hand-warming and heart-warming energizer participants applaud their accomplishments and give each other a standing ovation.

GOALS

1) To boost group energy.

2) To promote affirmation as a stress management strategy.

GROUP SIZE

Unlimited

TIME FRAME

2 minutes

PROCESS

Note: This exercise has a powerful impact when repeated several times during a workshop or session.

1) The trainer asks the group to warm up their hands by applauding something or someone they are grateful for (eg, conference organizing committee, the cooks, a winning football team, an approaching holiday, what they've learned in the course, their family or friends, etc).

    Note: In this first round, the trainer should either specify the target of appreciation or ask for suggestions from the group and choose one.

2) The trainer asks people to think of another target for their appreciation and once again provide a round of applause. As the clapping gains momentum, the trainer leads the group into a standing ovation, exhorting participants to whistle, cheer, stamp and shout with reckless abandon!

VARIATION

■ In Step 2, participants could request a standing ovation for themselves or nominate someone else in the group for a heart-warming experience. In either case, the person making the suggestion should state why the recipient needs or deserves the applause.

68 SEAWEED AND OAK

Participants alter their energy flow, using fantasy to become as flexible as floating seaweed and as sturdy as an oak tree.

GOALS

1) To become aware of how thoughts and energy flow are interrelated.

2) To compare spontaneity and control in two contrasting experiences of relaxation.

GROUP SIZE

Unlimited

TIME FRAME

5-10 minutes

MATERIALS NEEDED

"Seaweed and Oak" instructions.

PROCESS

1) The trainer introduces the exercise, inviting participants to join him in experiencing two types of mind and body relaxation. He reads the "Seaweed and Oak Instructions."

2) The trainer facilitates a group discussion regarding situations when spontaneity and control are most appropriate, asking questions like:

   □ When is it more appropriate to be spontaneous and flexible like the seaweed? (eg, on your birthday, running in the park, relaxing with friends, playing with the kids, etc)

   □ When is it more appropriate to be strong and controlled like the oak? (eg, before an exam or job interview, during a confrontation, performance, etc)

VARIATION

■ This exercise can be done in dyads. One person stands behind the other. The person in front closes her eyes and follows the instructions as read by the trainer (or her

partner). The person behind plays the ocean (for the seaweed) and the wind (for the oak tree) gently pushing his
partner's shoulders from side to side to test her energy
flow and heighten her awareness of her responses.

SEAWEED AND OAK INSTRUCTIONS

Stand comfortably with arms relaxed at your sides, knees un-
locked, eyes closed. Slowly shift your weight from side to side.

Think about a piece of seaweed, firmly attached to the ocean
floor but free to move gently with the movement of the water.
Focus your attention above your head and imagine becoming that
piece of seaweed, drifting, floating, moving easily and freely,
changing form with the tide and the current, feeling light and
relaxed.

Come back to the center and open your eyes. Then close your
eyes again.

Think about a strong oak tree in the forest with firm roots growing deep into the earth. Focus your attention into your abdomen
and imagine becoming that oak tree. Feel your roots growing down
your legs, out through the bottom of your feet into the ground.
Feel a strong connection with the earth beneath you. You are
strong and sturdy and secure. Although the wind may move your
branches, you are very safe in a storm. You are grounded and
centered, feeling your inner strength, feeling firm and relaxed.

Submitted by Martha Belknap

69 STRESS STRETCHERS

This quick energizer uses rubberbands to illustrate the
tension/relaxation dynamics of stress and to demonstrate
the need for creativity in coping.

GOALS

1) To illustrate the individuality of healthy stress and
   tension levels.

2) To get the creative juices flowing and prepare participants for expanding their coping skill repertoire.

3) To laugh, have fun and relieve the tension of talking
   about stress.

GROUP SIZE

Unlimited; 20-35 works well.

TIME FRAME

5-10 minutes maximum; keep the pace moving.

MATERIALS NEEDED

Bags of rubberbands -- mixed colors and sizes.

PROCESS

*Note: This exercise makes an excellent transition from a
         stress identification/assessment process to a coping
         skills presentation.*

1) The trainer sets a light, playful mood while she introduces the exercise as a transition from stress identi-
   fication to coping strategies. She passes the bag of
   rubberbands around the group, telling each person to
   take one.

2) Participants are invited to explore and comment on the
   effect of tension on their rubberbands. The trainer
   guides the process and asks facilitative questions:

   □ Stretch the rubberband, what happens? (eg, gets
     thin, gets tight, might break, etc)

   □ Relax the tension, what happens? (eg, nothing,
     gets floppy, etc)

☐ Put it between your teeth and pull on the other end.
Find the right balance of stretch so that it makes
pleasing music. Twang away.

The trainer comments on the similarity between people
and rubberbands -- with just the right amount of tension, we make beautiful music!

3) The trainer asks participants to brainstorm all the uses
of a rubberband (eg, make music, chew it to relieve
tension, use as slingshot to keep people away, organize
things together, repair broken toy, as a reminder around
the wrist, to decorate, to tie up hair, etc).

The trainer points out the similarity of the rubberband
to effective stress management skills (eg, need to be
flexible, need to have multiple uses, need to be creative, skills need to change with situations, need at
times to stretch and grow, etc).

4) The trainer praises participants for their creativity
and suggests that they will find the same success in
designing their own stress management program.

5) The trainer recommends that people keep their rubberbands in pocket or purse (or around their wrists) as a
cue to remind them of something they learned during
this session (eg, "When I see my rubberband, I'll take
a deep breath" or "When I notice my rubberband, I'll
remind myself to be flexible", etc).

TRAINER'S NOTES

Submitted by Sally Strosahl

70 TARGET PRACTICE

Participants choose a coping skill and experiment with using it during a coffee or lunch break.

GOALS

1) To visualize where, when and how a specific stress management strategy might be useful.

2) To practice a new or under-utilized coping skill.

GROUP SIZE

Unlimited

TIME FRAME

10 minutes

PROCESS

Note: This exercise works best just before a scheduled break and when preceded by a coping skills assessment, such as PILEUP COPERS (p 54), THE AAAbc's OF STRESS MANAGEMENT (Stress I, p 49) or COPING SKILLS ASSESSMENT (Stress I, p 63).

1) The trainer invites participants to join in a stress management experiment. She asks each person to pick a coping skill he would like to develop more fully (eg, assertiveness, contact, positive self-talk, humor, surrender, play, exercise, value clarification, listening, etc). Participants write down the target skill.

2) The trainer asks participants two questions about implementing this skill, allowing plenty of time for people to silently image their responses:

□ Concentrate on this skill you would like to improve. Imagine how you would act using that skill effectively to manage some of the stress in your life. Where would you especially like to try it? When? Picture yourself using the skill expertly in a stressful situation.

□ Now, I'd like you to imagine how you would act here at this workshop/class if you were using this skill effectively. How could this skill be implemented right here and now?

3)   The trainer announces a coffee break and challenges
     participants to practice their target skills. They are
     to use that skill and that skill only during the entire
     break time, acting as if they were already proficient
     and comfortable with the technique.

4)   After the break, the trainer invites reports from par-
     ticipants on what they experienced during this practice
     session.

TRAINER'S NOTES

71 TEN SECOND BREAK

Participants learn a ten second breathing and auto-
suggestion break that's ideal for instant stress relief.

GOALS

1) To interrupt or prevent tension build-up.

GROUP SIZE

Unlimited

TIME FRAME

5 minutes

MATERIALS NEEDED

"Ten Second Break" handouts for everyone.

PROCESS

1) The trainer solicits from the group examples of stressful situations when they would like a reliable "instant"
stress relief technique (eg, exams, arguments, when
irritated, when hassled, when anxious, etc).

2) The trainer distributes the "Ten Second Break" handouts
and informs participants that this simple exercise can
be a lifesaver for stressful situations. He describes
and demonstrates the technique following the instructions on top of the handout and then leads the group
through several practice routines.

   The trainer points out that if time does not permit a
   full ten second break, Step 3 alone is often an effective stopgap measure.

3) Participants are encouraged to try this ten second
break whenever they are irritated -- no matter how small
an irritation. It also can give them "breathing room"
in conflict situations where they are trying to decide
what to do or how to act.

4) The trainer points out that a frequent source of stress
for many people is the telephone. He teaches the group
the modified sequence for phone calls as described on
the handout.

TEN SECOND BREAK

<u>Basic Routine</u>

STEP 1   Smile as you think to yourself

              "My body doesn't need this _____"
                                          (irritation or stress)

STEP 2   Take a slow, deep <u>belly</u> breath --

              Count to 4 slowly on inhale and on exhale

STEP 3   Take a second deep belly breath --

              Close your eyes at the top of the inhalation.

              As you exhale imagine (visualize or feel)
              something warm entering your body at your head
              and flowing down into your hands and feet.

              Heaviness and warmth are flowing in.
              Think the phrase, <u>"I am calm."</u>

STEP 4   Open your eyes.

<u>Modified Routine for Phone Calls</u>

STEP A   When the phone <u>begins to ring</u>:

              Do STEP 3 first -- then answer the phone.

STEP B   <u>During</u> the phone call:

              Relax shoulders and jaw.
              Breathe from your abdomen as rhythmically as
              possible.

STEP C   <u>After</u> the phone call:

              Do the complete "Ten Second Break," STEPS 1-4.

72 TREASURE CHEST

In this colorful guided fantasy participants discover a treasure chest containing a "gift" they need.

GOALS

1) To synthesize and "own" what has been learned during the session.

GROUP SIZE

Unlimited

TIME FRAME

15-20 minutes

PROCESS

1) The trainer invites participants to experience a guided fantasy that will provide a relaxing wrap-up to any segment of a session or course. She reads the "Treasure Chest Fantasy" script, customizing the instructions to fit the group situation and course content to be high-lighted.

Note: Before beginning the fantasy, the trainer will need to decide what "gift" she wants participants to discover in the treasure chest. The "gift" can be related to the overall goals of the course (eg, the gift of what you need to manage your stress better) or it can be tied to the specific topic of this session (eg, the gift of relaxation or assertiveness or a positive outlook, etc).

2) Participants pair up and describe the "gifts" they discovered. (5 minutes)

TRAINER'S NOTES

Submitted by J J Cochran

Treasure Chest Fantasy

Put your feet flat on the floor . . . scoot your seat against the back of the chair . . . place your hands comfortably in your lap.

Take a deep breath . . . let it go . . . take another deep breath . . . let it go . . . take another deep breath . . . Close your eyes . . . Let your body relax . . . allow yourself to breathe deeply and heavily . . . as you inhale, inhale relaxation . . . as you exhale, exhale tension . . . Allow yourself to be calm and relaxed.

Now imagine yourself in a field of red . . . run through the field of red . . . see the poppies . . . see the cardinals . . . Allow yourself to experience red.
   Note: Let people experience "red" for about 45 seconds.

Then go into a field of orange . . . allow yourself to experi-ence orange . . . see the oranges . . . see the orange flowers . . . Allow yourself the experience of the field of orange . . . allow yourself to smell it . . . What does it taste like?
   Note: Again wait for approximately 45 seconds.

Now imagine yourself in a field of yellow. See the yellow flowers . . . see the daises and daffodils . . . see the canaries . . . and anything else yellow . . . Totally experience yellow . . . What does it sound like? . . . What does it feel like? . . . Immerse yourself in yellow.
   Note: Wait 45 seconds.

Then go into a field of green . . . experience the incredible number of shades of green . . . Let the green surround you . . . experience the field of green.
   Note: Wait 45 seconds.

Imagine yourself in a field of blue, sky blue . . . allow your-self to relax in blue . . . see the blue flowers . . . breathe in the blueness . . . Experience what blue feels like.
   Note: Wait 45 seconds.

Now imagine a field of dark blue, indigo . . . see the bluebirds . . . see the blueberries . . . surround yourself with that dark blue . . . Allow that dark blue to surround you . . . What does it taste like? . . . What does it smell like?
   Note: Wait 45 seconds.

Then imagine yourself in a field of purple, deep royal purple . . . see the violets . . . see the other purple flowers . . . Let yourself experience the purple . . . what it feels like . . . what it sounds like . . . what it tastes like.
   Note: Wait 45 seconds.

Now imagine that all the colors become one and turn into a white light surrounding you . . . let the white light penetrate and envelope you.

Now you notice you're on a path in a forest . . . allow yourself to walk through the forest . . . until you become aware that you're coming to a clearing . . . There's a pond in the clearing . . . by the pond is your favorite tree . . . Let yourself sit by the tree . . . and think about *(the topic)* .
>   Note: *Insert a topic relevant to the course such as "stress,"*
>   *"relationships," "humor," "worrying," "grief,"*
>   *"health," "coping," etc.*

The pond is clear and deep . . . you can see the bottom . . . and you notice a chest is at the bottom of the pond.

Now imagine yourself -- even if you can't swim, it's okay, you're safe . . . just imagine yourself diving into the pond and bringing up the treasure chest . . . bring it back over to where you are by the tree.

In just a minute, I'll ask you to open the treasure chest . . . Inside there will be a gift regarding *(the chosen topic)* . . . The gift will be a word . . . or a picture . . . or a thought . . . or a presence . . . Don't try to make anything happen . . . just let it come to you . . . if you don't get something during this process . . . just let that be okay . . . it will come to you later on today . . . or in your sleep.

Now, open the box . . . and see what gift is inside . . . and let the gift talk to you . . . telling you what it is for and what it means.
>   Note: *Wait approximately 30 seconds.*

If you have any questions, ask the gift now.
>   Note: *Wait approximately 30 seconds.*

Now you have a choice . . . In just a minute, I'll ask you to do one of two things . . . You can either close the box and put it back in the water . . . or . . . you can put your hands out in front of you . . . and imagine the treasure chest shrinking . . . shrinking small enough to fit into your hands. . . Then imagine opening your heart . . . and putting the treasure chest inside your heart for safe-keeping . . . Do one of those right now.
>   Note: *Wait 30 seconds.*

Now, get up and start walking along the path . . . and count from 1 to 5 . . . when you get to 5, you'll be back in this room.

CONTRIBUTORS

Martha Belknap MA
Educational Consultant
395 Monroe
Denver CO 80206
303/321-0905

Marti is an educational consultant with a speciality in creative relaxation and stress management skills. She has 25 years of teaching experience at all levels. Marti offers relaxation workshops and creativity courses through schools, universities, hospitals and businesses.

Thomas G Boman PhD
Professor, Dept of
  Professional Education
U of Minnesota-Duluth
Duluth MN 55812
218/726-7157 (campus)
218/724-2317 (home)

Tom is a practicing educator, inservice trainer and program developer. His role as founder of the Society for Orthosynergistic Behavior (the study of the right combination of behaviors to enhance high level well-being) allows him ample opportunity to study the maintaining of professional and personal vitality. PhD in Educational Psychology, MA in Curriculum and Instruction, BS in Chemistry.

Sandy Christian MSW
Clinical Supervisor
Lutheran Social Service
219 North 6th Avenue East
Duluth MN 5805
218/728-3916 (office)

Sandy is a creative marriage and family therapist who has for 15 years avoided the high burnout rate of her profession by sprinkling a large dose of teaching and peer support networking into her busy life. She is currently discovering the abiding eustress and occasional distress of being a parent, as well as a social worker.

J J Cochran
President
The Grand Opening --
makes your convention work
4022 Pillsbury
Minneapolis MN 55409
612/825-8437

J J specializes in designing interaction exercises for large groups which create an atmosphere conducive to participation, information exchange and achieving convention goals. Daylong seminar on "self-image and impact". Keynotes and workshops on "personal empowerment and personal power".

Joel Goodman EdD
Director
The Humor Project
110 Spring Street
Saratoga Springs NY 12866
518/587-8770

Joel has been an advocate of exper-
iential education since his grad-
uate school days at U Mass during
the early '70's. Author of several
books ranging from values clarification to magic, Joel helps folks
get serious about humor through
workshops, speeches and the journal
he edits, "Laughing Matters!"

Gloria Singer ACSW
Center For Health Management
101 West 2nd Street
Duluth MN 55802
218/727-4167 (office)

Gloria's background as a social
worker and educator are valuable
assets in her position as Employee
Assistance Specialist at the Center
for Health Management. In that
capacity she has enjoyed designing
site-specific programs in stress
management and wellness as well as
training, counseling and group work
with employees and their families.

Mary O'Brien Sippel RN MS
517 Lincoln Park Drive
Duluth MN 55806
218/723-6130 (office)
218/722-8136 (home)

Mary is still one of Whole Person
Associates' most enthusiastic faculty. Now a counselor and faculty
member at the College of St Scholastica, Mary continues to inspire
others to care for themselves and
stay vital. Mary's experience in
teaching stress management across
the country has enabled her to be
her own best caretaker as career
woman, wife and mother of two
toddlers.

Sally Strosahl MA
Marriage & Family Therapist
436 Watson
Aurora IL   60505
312/851-4446 (office)

Sally has an MA in clinical psychology; trained at the Wholistic
Health Center; researched the relationship between stress and illness.
In addition to her private practice
in marriage and family therapy,
Sally frequently presents workshops
in the areas of stress management,
burnout, support groups, parenting
and combining career and mother-
hood. She particularly enjoys
working with "systems" (family,
work groups, agencies, business,
churches) to help enhance each member's growth and well-being.

David X Swenson PhD
Dir of Student Development
College of St Scholastica
1200 Kenwood Avenue
Duluth MN 55811
218/724-6903 (home)
218/723-6085 (office)

A licensed psychologist, Dave main-
tains a private practice in addition to his administrative, educational and therapeutic roles at the
college. He provides consultation
and training to human services,
health and law enforcement agencies.
Dave has been a student of the mar-
tial arts for 20 years.

Randy R Weigel
Human Development Specialist
Iowa State University
213 Child Development
Ames IA 50011
515/294-8754 (office)

Through workshops, study guides
and media development, Randy specializes in making stress research
understandable and usable by lay
audiences. His training in human
relations and education allows him
to tailor programs to the needs of
specific audiences. Randy has
trained students, faculty, parents,
farmers and helping professionals
in stress management.

Genie L Wessel RN MS
Coordinator
Administrative Staff
Howard Co Health Department
Ellicott City MD 21043
301/992-2369 (office)

Genie is a community health nurse
now functioning in a Staff Support
position to the local Health Offi-
cer. She is involved in program
planning for employees and the
community. Genie has offered programs in stress reduction, employee
wellness and a special program for
women returning to school. She
works through the Health Department
and various local organizations.

© 1984 Whole Person Press   PO Box 3151   Duluth MN 55803

THE EDITORS

All Handbook exercises not specifically documented are the creative efforts of the editors who have been designing, collecting
and experimenting with structured processes in their teaching,
training and consultation work since the late 1960's.

Nancy Loving Tubesing, EdD, holds a masters degree in group counseling and a doctorate in counselor education. She served as
editor of the Society for Wholistic Medicine's monograph series
and articulated the principles of whole person health care in
the monograph, Philosophical Assumptions. A Faculty Associate
and Publications Director at Whole Person Associates, Nancy is
currently channeling her creative energies into the development
of the Handbook series and the compilation and testing of exercises for future volumes.

Donald A Tubesing, MDiv, PhD, designer of the widely acclaimed
STRESS SKILLS seminar and author of Kicking Your Stress Habits,
has been a pioneer in the movement to reintegrate the body, mind
and spirit in health care delivery. With his background in psychology, theology and education, Don brings the whole person
perspective to his consultation in business and industry, government agencies and hundreds of health care and human service
systems.

Nancy and Don have collaborated on many writing projects over
the years, beginning with a small group college orientation project in 1970 and culminating in the publication of their new
self-help book on whole person wellness, The Caring Question
(Minneapolis: Augsburg, 1983).

FUTURE CONTRIBUTORS

If you develop an exciting, effective structured exercise you'd like to share with other trainers in the field of stress management or wellness promotion, please send it to us for consideration using the following guidelines:

1) *Your entry should be written in a format similar to those in this Handbook.*

2) *Contributors must either guarantee that the materials they submit are not previously copyrighted or provide a copyright release for inclusion in the Whole Person Handbook series.*

3) *When you have adapted from the work of others, please acknowledge the original source of ideas or activities.*

4) *Include a brief (40 words) creative biography similar to those above.*

All contributors will be acknowledged on receipt. The editors will review each submission and test it with one or more groups before reaching a decision about inclusion. Materials must be received by July 1st to be considered for the next year's Handbook volume. You will be notified by October 1st whether or not your exercise will be included.

WHOLE PERSON PUBLICATIONS

KICKING YOUR STRESS HABITS:
A do-it-yourself guide for coping with stress

by Donald A Tubesing, MDiv, PhD

Striking graphics highlight this unusual "workshop-in-a-book" which actively engages readers in identifying sources of stress and resources for coping. Full of examples, worksheets, checklists, practical ideas and a planning process that really works! Ideal for classroom or group setting. Large format paperback, $10.00

THE CARING QUESTION
You first or me first — choosing a healthy balance

by Donald A Tubesing & Nancy Loving Tubesing

Thought-provoking questions are scattered throughout this startling challenge to the wellness revolution. Filled with wit and wisdom, The Caring Question invites readers to move beyond wellness to a life that balances self-care with caring for others. Paperback, $3.95.

WHOLE PERSON HEALTH CARE: Philosophical Assumptions

by Nancy Loving Tubesing

This slim volume is packed with insights concerning the nature and form of whole person health care along with snapshots of the theory in practice, challenges to practitioners, and suggestions for research. Paperback, $6.00.

IN OUR OWN HANDS
A woman's book of self-help therapy

by Sheila Ernst and Lucy Goodison

This practical guidebook for starting a self-help group belongs in the library of every professional who works with groups. Clear, concise descriptions of several theoretical approaches are interspersed with oodles of outstanding exercises that any group could try. Add 143 techniques to your bag of tricks. Paperback, $9.95

© 1984 Whole Person Press PO Box 3151 Duluth MN 55803

TAPE/WORKBOOK TRAINING PACKAGES

STRESS SKILLS: A structured strategy for helping people manage stress more effectively

Voice-over narration guides the listener through the celebrated STRESS SKILLS seminar experience captured in these recordings. Concept essays precede each worksheet in the Participant Workbook and highlight topics such as: the nature of stress, taking control of stress, choice and change, whole person stress analysis and 20 stress skills. Perfect for individual or small group study, this resource would be a valuable addition to any staff training library. Six cassettes with companion workbook, $75.00. Workbook only, $6.00.

TUNE IN: Empathy training workshop

TUNE IN is a carefully developed and extensively tested empathy training workshop you can conduct yourself. The 16 hours of tape-led group experiences help participants develop competency in basic listening and empathy skills. Currently used around the world for inservice training of counselors, teachers, physicians, hospital personnel, volunteers, nurses, clergy, office staff, managers and administrators. Workshop tapes, Leader Manual and Participant Workbook, $75.00. Workbook only, $6.00.

Rx for BURNOUT: Promoting vitality and preventing burnout in the care-giving professions

Carefully edited, attractively packaged cassette recordings of a live, Rx for BURNOUT workshop can be used with the accompanying Participant Workbook to create the seminar atmosphere and process. Topics include: symptoms, stages and causes; stress/vitality in the workplace; individual revitalization strategies; interpersonal support networking and planning for renewal. Order this package for conducting your own workshop or to share with friends and colleagues. Tapes and workbook, $75.00. Workbook only, $6.00

UNUSUAL CASSETTE TAPES

RELAX . . . LET GO . . . RELAX

Music by Steven Halpern provides the calming background for a 30
minute "end of the day" relaxation sequence for shedding tension,
and a 20 minute "anytime of the day" revitalization routine.
Male and female narration, $9.00.
Also available without music, $7.50.

SPIRITUAL CENTERING: An inward journey of renewal

In this non-judgmental exploration of personal spiritual depths,
Don Tubesing guides listeners through a process of quieting and
centering that allows each person to discover her own internal
wisdom. Useful as a discussion starter or closing motivator.
Flip side with Halpern Sounds musical background. Tape in
holder, $9.00.

FINGERTIP FACE MASSAGE: A gentle self care break

In her warm and gentle manner, Mary O'Brien Sippel guides listeners through a refreshing self-massage process. The 10-minute
experience generates a feeling of relaxation, well-being and re-
newed vitality. Use this tape as an "energy break" during long
sessions or to kick off your presentation of self-care options.
Flip side with Halpern Sounds musical background. Tape in
holder, $9.00.

YOU ALONE CAN BE WELL . . . But you can't be well alone!

In this keynote speech from Wellness Promo VII, Dr Donald Tubesing
addresses the issue of wellness from the whole person perspective,
asking the question, "What's the point of being well?" Listeners
are asked to reflect on the self/other care balance in their
lives. A humorous, challenging, positive 90 minutes. Tape in
holder, $9.00.

BEYOND PEPTALKS AND HANDOUTS

Effective teaching helps people move beyond information to implementation. In this practical presentation, process education
expert Dr Don Tubesing shares his philosophy and time-tested
techniques for getting participants involved in the learning
experience. Tape in holder, $9.00.

THE WHOLE PERSON HANDBOOKS
for trainers, educators and group leaders

STRUCTURED EXERCISES IN STRESS MANAGEMENT

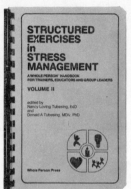

Nancy Loving Tubesing, EdD and
Donald A Tubesing, PhD, Editors

Volume I (orange cover) contains 36 ready-to-
use teaching designs that involve the participant as a whole person in learning to manage
stress more effectively. These exercises help
motivate people to identify desired changes,
build new coping skills and plan for a health-
ier lifestyle.

This practical resource includes icebreakers,
stress assessments, management strategies,
skill builders, action planners and group
energizers. Spiral bound, flexible plastic
cover, $15.95

Volume II (red cover) contains 36 all new
process teaching ideas in the same easy-to-
use format. $15.95

STRUCTURED EXERCISES IN WELLNESS PROMOTION

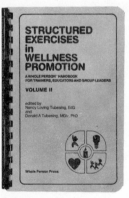

Nancy Loving Tubesing, EdD and
Donald A Tubesing, PhD, Editors

Volume I (green cover) includes 36 experien-
tial learning activities that focus on whole
person health -- body, mind, spirit, emotions,
relationships. These exercises encourage
people to adopt a wellness-oriented attitude
and develop more responsible self-care patterns.

This handy volume contains icebreakers, wellness explorations, self-care strategies,
action planners and group energizers. Spiral
bound, soft plastic cover, $15.95.

Volume II (blue cover) includes 36 totally
different individual and group exercises
that promote wellness. $15.95.

THE STRESS KIT

Whole Person Press is proud to announce the latest innovation in stress management resources — a multimedia kit that stresses creative coping. Designed by Whole Person Associates as a health promotion tool for a major insurance company, **The Stress Kit** is now available for your personal or professional use.

The kit includes three educational components — PILEUP (a card game), The Stress Examiner (an unusual newspaper) and Stress Talk/StressRelease (cassette tape programs). This $45.80 value is available packaged together in an attractive bookshelf container for only $29.95. The components may also be purchased separately.

Use one or more of these fun-filled pieces with staff, clients, students, team members, family or friends. You'll understand stress better — and discover positive, effective coping strategies.

PILEUP

A deck of 108 colorful stress and coping cards with instructions for 12 self-discovery games. Card sorts, role plays, assessments, simulations and games graphically demonstrate how stress piles up and how creativity can expand your coping capabilities. Super for families or work teams! $15.95 separately.

The Stress Examiner

This 12-page, 4-color newspaper (USA Today format) is bursting with information and activities for readers of all ages. Test your stress quotient. Play Penny Pileup. Read how celebrities cope. Find out about stress and how to deal with it in every day situations. A book-full of ideas — yet so much more readable! $3.95 separately.

Stress Talk/StressRelease

Side A (Stress Talk) of this tape provides a mini-workshop that guides an individual or group in exploring personal stress patterns and management styles. Reproducible worksheets are included for group use. $15.95 separately.

Side B (Stress Release) features a special "radio broadcast" that teaches simple, effective techniques to relieve tension. The program ends with a 15-minute progressive relaxation exercise, complete with mood music. $9.95 separately.

ORDER FORM

Name _____

Address _____

_____

City _____

State _____ Zip _____

Please make checks payable and send to:
Whole Person Associates Inc
PO Box 3151
Duluth MN 55803
218/728-4077

WHOLE PERSON HANDBOOKS for trainers, educators & group leaders

Structured Exercises in Stress Management
☐ Volume I (orange cover, 1983)..................... 15.95 _____
☐ Volume II (red cover, 1984)....................... 15.95 _____

Structured Exercises in Wellness Promotion
☐ Volume I (green cover, 1983)...................... 15.95 _____
☐ Volume II (blue cover, 1984) .... 15.95 _____

TAPE/WORKBOOK TRAINING PACKAGES
☐ STRESS SKILLS workshop......................... 75.00 _____
☐ TUNE IN workshop............................... 75.00 _____
☐ Rx for BURNOUT workshop........................ 75.00 _____

WORKBOOKS ONLY
☐ STRESS SKILLS Participant Workbook............. 6.00 _____
☐ TUNE IN Participant Workbook................... 6.00 _____
☐ Rx for BURNOUT Participant Workbook............ 6.00 _____

BOOKS
☐ Kicking Your Stress Habits..................... 10.00 _____
☐ The Caring Question........................... 3.95 _____
☐ Philosophical Assumptions..................... 6.00 _____
☐ Wholistic Health............................. 12.95 _____
☐ In Our Own Hands............................. 9.95 _____

TAPES
☐ Relax . . . Let Go . . . Relax................ 7.50 _____
☐ Relax . . . Let Go . . . Relax (with Halpern Sounds)........... 9.00 _____
☐ Spiritual Centering........................... 9.00 _____
☐ Fingertip Face Massage........................ 9.00 _____
☐ You Alone Can Be Well . . . But You Can't Be Well Alone!....... 7.50 _____
☐ Beyond Pep Talks and Handouts .... 9.00 _____
☐ **THE STRESS KIT**............................ 29.95 _____
  ☐ StressTalk (cassette workshop)............. 15.95 _____
  ☐ Pile Up (educational card game)............ 15.95 _____
  ☐ StressRelease (radio program cassette)..... 9.95 _____
  ☐ The Stress Examiner (newspaper)............ 3.95 _____

☐ My check is enclosed (US funds only)

☐ Please charge my bank card

   ☐ VISA   ☐ Mastercard

   Card # _____

   Expiration date _____

   Signature _____

☐ Bill my institution (PO # _____)

SUBTOTAL _____
TAX (MN residents 6%) _____
*SHIPPING _____
GRAND TOTAL _____

*Shipping. We ship UPS in the US. Please include $2.50 for the first item and 50¢ for each additional item. Outside the continental US please add $4.00.